DAD JOKES TOO

See what we did there?

PUNNIER THAN EVER

WARNING: Contains more than 800 NEW eye-rollers, sidesplitters, knee-slappers, and gut-busters guaranteed to make you laugh...or sigh.

Editors of Portable Press

PORTABLE
PRESS

San Diego, California

Portable Press
An imprint of Printers Row Publishing Group
10350 Barnes Canyon Road, Suite 100, San Diego, CA 92121
www.portablepress.com • mail@portablepress.com

Printers Row Publishing Group is a division of Readerlink Distribution Services, LLC. Portable Press is a registered trademark of Readerlink Distribution Services, LLC.

Correspondence regarding the content of this book should be sent to Portable Press, Editorial Department, at the above address.

Publisher: Peter Norton • Associate Publisher: Ana Parker
Senior Developmental Editor: April Graham Farr
Developmental Editor: Vicki Jaeger
Production Team: Jonathan Lopes, Rusty von Dyl

Editor and Project Manager: J. Carroll
Content Curation: Brian Boone, Josh Novey, J. Carroll
Interior Design: Susan Engbring
Cover Concept: Michael Sherman
Cover: SunDried Penguin

Library of Congress Control Number: 2019957609
ISBN: 978-1-68412-953-9

Printed in the United States of America

24 23 22 21 20   1 2 3 4 5

CONTENTS

THE DAILY GRIND
Work, School, and Other Necessary Evils

Q: What does a new dad who hates 9-to-5 jobs do?
A: He goes out and gets a 9-to-5 job is what.

I tried to write a novel, but it didn't work out.
I guess I didn't have the write stuff.

A set of jumper cables goes into a bar. "Can I get a drink?" the cables ask.

"Okay," the bartender replies. "But don't start anything."

Q: What's the definition of *meeting*?
A: A wasted hour full of useless info that could've been covered in an e-mail.

Q: Why do dog trainers have long-lasting marriages?
A: Because they know how to get someone to *stay*.

I've been to war. I've raised twins. If I had a choice, I'd rather go to war.

—George W. Bush

A man walks into a clothing shop and says, "Hi, I'd like to try on that slick suit in the store window."

"Sure," the clerk replies, "but wouldn't you be more comfortable using a dressing room?"

Interviewer: What would you say is your greatest weakness?
Applicant: Probably differentiating between reality and fantasy. Sometimes it's hard to

know what's really possible and what's just a pipe dream.
Interviewer: Okay. What are your strengths?
Applicant: I was born on the planet Krypton, which gives me super-strength and the ability to fly.

Q: When do sailors stop playing cards?
A: When their captain is on deck.

What dads say: "Sorry, can't talk—I've got to leave for an early meeting."
What dads mean: "I don't want to have this awkward conversation right now."

Q: Why can't you lie to X-ray technicians?
A: Because they can see right through you.

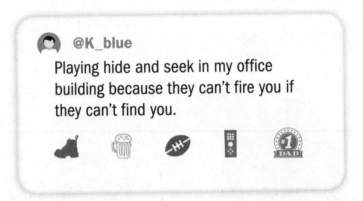

@K_blue

Playing hide and seek in my office building because they can't fire you if they can't find you.

One day, a teacher sent the class trouble-maker to the principal's office. "Do you know why you're here?" asked the principal.

Hesitating, the kid asked, "Because of this morning?"

"Yes," the principal said sternly. "Your teacher says you ran in the hall, hit two students, started a food fight in the cafeteria, and cursed at one of your classmates."

"Boy, that's a relief," the student said with a sigh. "I thought you found out I broke your car windshield."

Q: How do farmers keep track of their livestock?
A: With a cowculator.

When the boss is out on vacation

A man walked into a bar and ordered a fruit punch. The bartender said, "If you want a fruit punch, you'll have to stand in line." The man looked around, but there was no punchline.

Knock-knock!
Who's there?
Cain.
Cain who?
Cain you have management decide what
they want *before* you have me run in circles
redoing work multiple times only to decide
it was fine the way it was and you
don't need my services after all?

An artist friend of mine asked me how I liked
his self-portrait. I told him that it was good,
except the eyebrows were too low and too
close together.
He seemed angry!

Did you hear about the butcher who got behind in his work?

Poor guy slipped, fell, and got his rear end stuck in the meat grinder.

Boss: Where do you see yourself in five years?
Employee: I'm just trying to make it to Friday, man.

Q: How do you keep your newspaper from flying away in the wind?
A: Use a news anchor.

A man was lying in the street, unconscious and bleeding. A psychologist who happened to be passing by rushed up to him and exclaimed, "My God! Whoever did this really needs help!"

Great Moments in Dad History

October 28, 1960. Dave Gordon grabs his keys on the way out of the house and becomes the first dad in history to say to his kids, "You ready to rock and roll?"

Q: What's a good name for a mountain climber?
A: Cliff.

Knock-knock!
Who's there?
Kent.
Kent who?
Kent you tell who this is?

Son: Dad, what do you do for a living?
Dad: Son, I'm not entirely sure.

Did you hear about the two guys who stole a calendar?

They each got six months.

Imagine how much worse meetings were back before you could pretend to take notes on your phone while you were really just messing around on Twitter.

 @ashleyn1cole

I have 80 unread emails and obviously the only solution is to chuck my computer into the sea.

Q: Why did the urologist lose his license?
A: He got in trouble with his peers.

Did you hear about the cowboy with dietary restrictions?
   He was rootin' tootin' free of gluten.

Q: Why did the detective stay in bed all day?
A: He was working undercover.

A police officer caught two kids playing with a car battery and a firework.
   He charged one and let the other one go.

Guy: What does your wife do for a living?
Friend: Well, it's difficult to say.
Guy: What do you mean?
Friend: Shelly sells seashells.
By the seashore.

Two guys are working on an assembly line. The first guy says, "I bet I can make the boss give me the day off."

The other man says, "I want the day off, too! But how?"

"Just watch." The first guy climbs on top of the machines and all the way up to the rafters. There, he swings his legs around and hangs upside down. Then he calls down to the boss, "Look at me!"

The boss exclaims, "What are you doing up there?"

The guy responds, "I'm a light bulb."

Shaking his head, the boss says, "Have you been working too hard? I think you're going crazy! Take the day off." As the employee climbs down, his cohort on the assembly line heads for the exit, too. "Why are *you* leaving?" the boss asks the second guy.

"Well," the man replies, "how am I supposed to work without lights?"

Q: How is apathy different from indifference?
A: Eh, who cares?

SOME OF DAD'S FAVORITE TOM SWIFTIES

"I used to own that gold mine,"
Tom ex-claimed.

"Measure twice before you cut,"
Tom remarked.

"Blow on the fire so it doesn't go out,"
Tom bellowed.

"Thanks for shredding the cheese,"
said Tom gratefully.

Q: Why does the Norwegian navy place bar
codes on all of its ships?
A: So it can scan the navy in.

Knock-knock!
Who's there?
Adair.
Adair who?
Adair once, but now I'm bald.

Child: Dad, what does the word "contemplate" mean?
Father: Think about it.
Child: Can't you just tell me?!

My boss told me I've been late three times this week. So I guess that means today is Wednesday.

"We get three wishes. Let's not waste them on something like 'Better coffee in the break room'."

Monday: Greg
Tuesday: Ian
Wednesday: Greg
Thursday: Ian
Friday: Greg

It's the Gregorian calendar.

The *Mission: Impossible* movies are a lot like my life. I'm just as stealthy as Tom Cruise's character when I try to leave my office at 5 p.m. without anyone seeing me and asking me a question.

Did you hear about the illegally parked frog?
  He got toad.

Customer: How much for a haircut?
Barber: Twenty dollars.
Customer: How about a shave?
Barber: Ten dollars.
Customer: Great. Shave my head.

My dog is a magician. He's a labracadabrador.

Knock-knock!
Who's there?
Wayne.
Wayne who?
The Wayne is really coming down out here!

One day during a rainstorm, a boss told an intern to water the plants outside the office. "But it's raining," the intern protested. The boss retorted, "Then take an umbrella!"

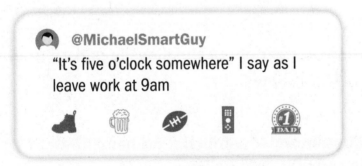

@MichaelSmartGuy

"It's five o'clock somewhere" I say as I leave work at 9am

Q: Why did the tech company hire a frog?
A: He was an excellent debugger.

Life insurance agent to a would-be client: Don't let me frighten you into a hasty decision. Sleep on it tonight. If you wake up in the morning, give me a call and let me know.

Patient: I think I'm a moth.
Dentist: You should see a psychiatrist, not a dentist.
Patient: I'm already seeing a psychiatrist.
Dentist: Then why are you here?
Patient: Your light was on.

Q: What candy do happy cowboys eat?
A: Jolly Ranchers.

A horse walks into a bar. "Hey!" yells the bartender.

"Yes, please!" replies the horse.

A sandwich walks into a bar. "Sorry," the bartender says, "we don't serve food here."

Q: What do you get if you rearrange the letters of *postman*?
A: A really ticked-off postman.

An art gallery owner approached an artist one day. "Good news," she told the artist. "A man came in today asking about two of your paintings and a sculpture."

"That's great! What did he want to know?"

The owner replied, "He was curious about whether your work would appreciate in value after your death."

"I suppose so. Did you get his contact info?" the artist asked.

"I didn't need to. He said he's your doctor."

The best part about conference calls is that you can multitask during them…as long as you remember to mute the phone. Especially when you flush.

A man goes to a toy store to get a Barbie doll for his kid. He asks the store clerk how much a Barbie costs.

The clerk says, "Doctor Barbie is $29.99, Gym Rat Barbie is $29.99, Latin America Barbie is $29.99, Beach Bum Barbie is $29.99, Party Barbie is $29.99, and Divorcée Barbie is $329.99."

"Whoa," the dad says. "Why is Divorcée Barbie over $300 when the rest are $29.99?"

"Divorcée Barbie comes with extra perks," the employee explains. "She's got Ken's house, Ken's beach hut, Ken's car, and Ken's boat."

I've been to the dentist a lot. I know the drill.

Q: Why did the truck driver finally stop farting?
A: He ran out of gas.

Boss: We need to talk about your workplace attire.
Employee: Why? Haven't you heard the phrase "dress for the job you want"?
Boss: Yes, but that doesn't mean you can come to work in a Spider-Man costume.

 @WoodyLuvsCoffee

Just waiting to see how long until my coworkers realize that my robbery story is just the lyrics to Gloria Gaynor's "I will Survive".

I don't burn bridges.
But I do fail to maintain them, and they structurally degrade over time.

Scientists were testing new compounds at a facility way out in the desert in Nevada. Unfortunately, there was a major biohazardous spill. Several countries came to the rescue. Russia, China, and Germany all sent state-of-the-art waste removal robots to help the U.S. robot clean up the site.

First, the Chinese robot broke down before it even reached the highly irradiated site. Then the American android worked in the zone for eight minutes before it, too, shut down. The German robot managed to clean for 20 minutes before finally succumbing to the immense heat and radiation. But during all this time, the Russian robot was hard at work, and the engineers from all the other nations watched in awe as it continued to remove waste for more than two hours.

A supervisor asked the Russian officer stationed there, "How is your robot still working after all this time?" The officer looked at them, glanced at the clock, and shouted over the communications system, "Private Anatoly! Come on out. Your shift is over."

I had to change the font in this letter I'm writing. It just wasn't my type.

BAD ADVICE FROM A REAL DAD

"Drive fast. The shorter the time you take to reach your destination, the less chance there is for you to get into an accident."

Kid: In class, we're studying different people's names and where they came from. Why is my sister named Daisy?
Dad: Because your mom's a gardener and loves flowers.
Kid: Oh! Thanks.
Dad: You got it, Sleeping in the Hammock.

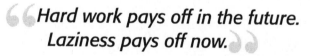
Hard work pays off in the future. Laziness pays off now.

—Steven Wright

Q: What's it called when a hospital doesn't have any maternity nurses available?
A: A mid-wife crisis.

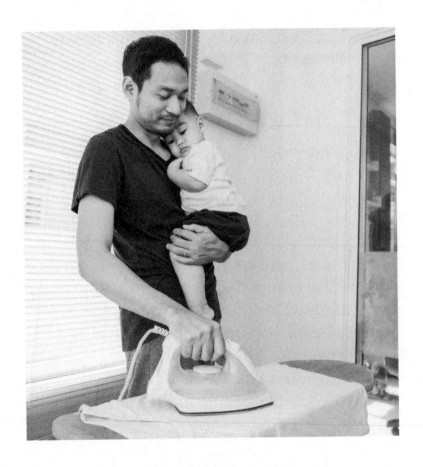

Knock-knock!
Who's there?
Harvey.
Harvey who?
Harvey having fun yet?

A truck driver noticed that cars kept cutting him off when he was trying to change lanes. He asked his passenger, "Hey, lean your head out the window to see if the turn signals are working."

The other guy did as he was asked. He reported, "Yes, no, yes, no, yes, no, yes, no..."

Q: Who makes the sandwiches for an office?
A: A sub committee.

Teen: I need a quick way to make some cold, hard cash.
Dad: Put your money in the freezer!

Q: What kind of snacks do firefighters eat?
A: Firecrackers.

Knock-knock!
Who's there?
Amos.
Amos who?
Amosquito just bit me!

Kid: Can I have a spare key?
Grandpa: Take the piano. It's got plenty of keys.

Q: Why did the reporter go to the ice cream shop?
A: He needed a scoop.

I tried to make reservations at the library. Unfortunately, they were booked.

Did you hear about the farmer who farted so explosively that it graced a thousand ears? That poor cornfield.

Kid: What would you do if your sock got a big hole in it?
Dad: I'd say, "Darn it!"

Knock-knock!
Who's there?
Gideon.
Gideon who?
Gideon up off your keister, and let's go!

Great Moments in Dad History

January 20, 1858. Edward Black becomes the first father ever to say "Can't complain!" when a coworker asks how he's doing.

Law firm partner: Would you say that you're honest?
Applicant: Let me explain it this way. My father lent me $100,000 for my education, and I paid back every penny the minute I tried my first case.
Partner: That's impressive. What was the case?
Applicant: My father sued me for $100,000.

I always wanted to be a Gregorian monk. But I never got the chants.

Q: What's the most secure and foul-smelling place in the United States?
A: Fart Knox.

Daughter: Can you help with my homework?
Dad: What subject?
Daughter: Geometry.
Dad: Gee, tree, I'm Dad!

Somebody blew up the Rogaine lab,
and now there's hair everywhere.
Police are combing the area.

"Please put some folds in these trousers,"
Tom pleaded.

 @Ndeshi_M

I told all my colleagues at work that I
have a twin so that when I see them in
public I don't have to talk to them.

Q: Why did the dumb guy fart at the
cemetery?
A: Because he saw a tombstone that read
"RIP."

Q: How do you know when trees are ready to
go home?
A: They leaf.

Q: What's the difference between your boss
and a mob boss?
A: The mob boss only requires you to kiss
his ring.

One evening, the airmen stationed at Area 51—the classified Air Force facility—were surprised to see a Cessna landing there. Immediately, the Military Police impounded the aircraft and hauled the pilot into an interrogation room. The pilot claimed his plane had a fuel leak and ran out of gas. Panicking, he had headed toward the only buildings in sight to make an emergency landing. The Air Force conducted a full background check on the pilot and held him overnight.

By the next day, the investigators believed the pilot's story and cleared him for release. After the plane was fixed and fueled, a lieutenant threatened the pilot with prison time if he ever told a soul that he'd been there, and the pilot flew away. The next day, however, the airmen were shocked to see the same Cessna land on base. Once again, the MPs surrounded the plane. This time, there were two people inside the craft. The same pilot jumped out with his hands up and said, "Do anything you want to me, but my wife is in the plane, and you have to tell her where I was last night!"

My computer's pop-up message said the password had to be eight characters long. So I picked Snow White and the Seven Dwarfs.

Q: Where does a tree keep all of its stuff?
A: In its trunk.

My father is named Bradley, and he found out his wife was pregnant on the same day he finished college.

That day was rad for dad grad Brad!

Q: What did the nose say to the finger?
A: "Stop picking on me!"

A man stood trial for robbery. The jury came back into the courtroom to return the verdict. The foreman stood and announced, "Not guilty."

The defendant leaped to his feet and shouted excitedly, "Does that mean I get to keep the money?"

 @House_Feminist

Please quit telling me to "keep up the good work" the good work was an accident and impossible to replicate

Q: What's a good name for a woman who set her credit card bill on fire?
A: Bernadette.

Q: What did one photon say to the other photon?
A: "I'm sick and tired of your interference!"

Q: What did the subatomic duck say?
A: "Quark!"

This museum I work for has
way too many fossils.
I have a bone to pick with them.

"We've taken over the government,"
Tom cooed.

Q: What do lawyers wear to court?
A: Lawsuits.

Crimes happen every day.
But the guy who got caught robbing
the bakery really takes the cake.

Daily Quotes for Dads

"Of all the titles I've been privileged to have, 'Dad' has always been the best."
—Ken Norton

THAT AND "BOWLING CHAMPION, 2004-2006."

Q: Why did the guy eat yeast and shoe polish before bed?
A: Because in the morning he wanted to rise and shine.

Knock-knock!
Who's there?
Rufus.
Rufus who?
Rufus covered in snow—let me in
before it slides down and buries me!

"I can see this making us more responsive to customers."

Q: Why did the cow jump over the moon?
A: The farmer had cold hands.

Q: How do you know hardcover books have mothers?
A: They're always wearing jackets.

Somebody really did a number in the office bathroom.

I got upset until I remembered that I work from home, and I'm the only one here.

A man walks into a supermarket and asks the clerk, "Can I get some candy for my kids?"

"Sorry," the clerk says, "we don't do exchanges."

My employees got me this reversible jacket.
I can't wait to see how it turns out!

Q: Why are seafood chefs so strong?
A: They've got a lot of mussels.

How hard is it for an astronaut to get life insurance? It's not rocket science!

A doctor and a lawyer meet at a party. As they try to chat, they're constantly interrupted. The other partygoers keep describing their medical problems to the doctor, wanting free advice. Finally, the frustrated doctor asks the lawyer, "How do you stop people from asking you for legal advice when you're not at work?"

"I give it to them," the lawyer says, "and then I mail them a bill."

The doctor decides to give it a try. A couple days later, he goes out to mail a stack of invoices to people who bothered him at the party. In his mailbox, he finds a bill from the lawyer.

"You dropped a stitch," Tom needled.

What dads say: "Sure, Boss, I'll have that to you first thing tomorrow."
What dads mean: "Sure, Boss, I'll have that to you at 4:59 p.m. tomorrow."

Q: Why did the polo player get thrown out of the match?
A: He was horsing around.

 @AbbyHasIssues

I've never wanted to know the answer to anything bad enough to ask a question at the end of a meeting that's running 30 minutes over time.

Q: How did the shoe salesman get his young daughter into an R-rated movie?
A: He had to sneaker in.

I'm one of 8/3 of people who will admit that they're bad at fractions.

I was going to nail a bookshelf to the wall. But then I thought to myself, "Oh, screw it."

Dad: Hey, before you go out there and sing tonight, let me give you a piece of advice.
Kid: What is it, Dad?
Dad: Don't forget a bucket.
Kid: Why?
Dad: To carry your tune!

Q: What grade did the eyeball get in math?
A: C.

Did you hear about the middle-schooler who had really smelly armpits?
   His teacher gave him an A because he never raised his hand in class.

Knock-knock!
Who's there?
Baldwin.
Baldwin who?
You'll be Baldwin you're older.

"The timeline has been shortened to 'Right now'."

"I suppose there's room for one more,"
Tom admitted.

Q: How is your workplace like a septic tank?
A: The biggest lumps always rise to the top.

Q: How did the mathematician resolve his constipation problem?
A: He worked it out with a pencil.

As a lumberjack, I know that I've cut exactly 2,417 trees.

I know because every time I cut one, I keep a log.

Q: Why's it so hard to work at McDonald's?
A: The boss is a clown.

By working faithfully eight hours a day, you may eventually get to be a boss and work 12 hours a day.

—Robert Frost

Adam's father died. While going through his father's possessions, Adam found a claim stub dated January 1986. Curious, he called the phone number and found that it was a shoe repair shop. Adam took the ticket there, and miraculously, the shop owner located a pair of leather loafers that belonged to his father. "Sorry, you can't take the shoes today," the owner said. "They'll be ready next week."

Q: How many managers does it take to change a light bulb?
A: Why don't you think about it, and we'll circle around later with an action plan at tomorrow's meeting, okay?

JoAnn never wanted her son to grow up to be a thief. But it's her own fault.
    She shouldn't have named him Rob.

Q: What class do snakes teach?
A: Hissssstory.

Q: Can an egg get into college?
A: Sure, if it passes the entrance eggs-am.

 @melowens
I wonder how many consecutive Mondays Todd will respond "not long enough" in regards to how his weekend was. We're at 7.

I went on vacation and haven't been to work in a week. When I return, I'll need retraining.
    I've completely forgotten how to play *Angry Birds*!

Q: Why did the football player buy a new lawn mower?
A: He had ten yards to go.

My fear of moving stairs isn't improving. If anything, it's escalating.

A man walks into a bar. Recognizing him, the bartender says, "Hey, I've got a great new joke for you!"

The NSA director smiles and replies, "Already heard it."

Q: What was left after an explosion at a French cheese factory?
A: Nothing but de brie.

Q: What do your supervisor and a bottle of beer have in common?
A: Both are empty from the neck up.

Q: Why is grandpa so wrinkled?
A: He hates being ironed.

Museum tour guide: This museum is full of art—
Dad: Then they better let Art out!

I'm so old I went to school with the Sun.
It got straight A's. It was so bright!

Q: Why were the teacher's eyes crossed?
A: His pupils were out of control.

My sister just married a taxi
cab driver. She was apparently
unaware of his checkered past.

Q: Why are pirate parties so dangerous?
A: Because they always go overboard.

Two boys are arguing in a classroom when their teacher walks in. "Whoa, whoa, what are you two fighting about?" she asks.

"We found a $10 bill on the ground, and we decided that whoever tells the biggest lie gets to keep it," one boy says.

"You should be ashamed of yourselves," the teacher replies. "When I was your age, I didn't even know what a lie was." The boys glance at each other, nod, and hand the $10 bill to the teacher.

A woman stopped being a nun after 20 years. She was ready to give up her habits.

Did you hear about the driver who ran into a truck full of strawberries?
Talk about a traffic jam.

Q: Why did the cartoon character have bad credit?
A: She was overdrawn.

Did you hear about the physics professor who dated a biology professor?

They ended their experiment. There was no chemistry.

I ran into an old friend the other day.
He's going to be fine, but my car is totaled.

Q: What did the atom say when
he lost an electron?
A: "Man, I really need to keep
an ion those things."

Q: How do you make a million dollars trading
penny stocks?
A: Start with two million dollars.

Knock-knock!
Who's there?
Impatient pirate.
Impatient pirate wh—
Arrrrrr!

Fishing in the ocean is serious work.
It's not something you do just for the halibut.

Somebody stole my sandwich out of the workplace fridge around 11 this morning! I got really mad until I realized I was full and didn't need lunch anyway...and it was because I'd already eaten that sandwich.

Q: Where's the fastest place to throw your garbage?
A: Into the dash can.

Q: Where's the best place to go Father's Day shopping?
A: Tie-Land.

I used to work at a pepper factory, but I quit. It was nothing to sneeze at.

Q: Why is lettuce so good at accounting?
A: It has a real head for it.

"Dolphins are highly intelligent," the aquarium tour guide said. "After just a few weeks in captivity, they can train humans to stand nearby and throw fish to them."

Great Moments in Dad History

April 5, 1978. Mike Ribecca becomes the first dad ever to say, "It must be free!" when a store clerk scans an item and it doesn't generate a price.

Q: Why did the old flashlight drop out of school?
A: It just wasn't very bright.

Did you hear about the clown who lived in the desert?
He had a dry sense of humor.

A cowboy walks into a bar. "What can I get for you?" the bartender asks.

"A double whiskey, neat," he replies.

As the bartender pours, she asks, "How's it going today?"

"I have a problem with my horses," the cowboy admits. "I want to train one of them to be a racehorse and the other to be a workhorse, but they look so similar I can't tell them apart!"

The bartender thinks it over for a minute and says, "How about you cut off one of their manes?"

"That's actually a great idea," the cowboy says.

One month later, the cowboy returns to the bar, looking depressed again. The bartender asks, "How are your horses?"

"The mane trick worked great at first, but then the hair grew back, and I can't tell them apart!"

She suggests, "Can you shave the hair off one of their tails?"

"That just might work..." the cowboy replies.

Another month passes. The cowboy returns, distraught. "Their tails and manes are the same length again!" he complains.

Exasperated, the bartender asks, "Can't you just measure their height or something?"

A week later, the cowboy runs in joyously and hugs the surprised bartender. "What's going on?" the bartender asks.

"It worked! The white horse is three inches taller than the black horse!"

A monastery opened up a fish-and-chips stand to earn money. One day, a customer came in and asked, "Are you the fish fryer?"

"No," the monk said. "I'm the chip munk."

To be indecisive, or not indecisive,
that is the question.
Or is it?

Did you hear about the fisherman magician?
He says, "Pick a cod, any cod!"

Knock-knock!
Who's there?
Aiken.
Aiken who?
Ow, my Aiken back!

 @TheCatWhisprer

The problem with teaching a man to fish is
that eventually somebody will microwave
that fish in the work break room.

Q: What do you call an Amish guy with his
hand stuck in a horse's mouth?
A: A mechanic.

A circus clown got sick and couldn't perform.
It was just a case of conjestion.

I used to be an accountant, from age 21 to 33. Then they fired me for no reason.
    What a complete waste of 18 years.

Did you hear about the army sergeant who was knocked down a rank?
    It was corporal punishment.

———

Q: What do you call twin police officers?
A: Copies.

Q: Why did the man quit the butcher training program?
A: He just couldn't cut it.

I used to run a coffee shop. Talk about a daily grind.

Curing cucumbers is tough.
One mistake and you wind up in a pickle.

Dad: Son, when Abraham Lincoln was your age, he walked 12 miles to school.
Son: Dad, when Abraham Lincoln was *your* age, he was president.

A mouse and her baby were wandering down an alley when a cat jumped out at them. The mother mouse shouted, "Woof!" and scared the cat away. "See?" the mom said. "That's why it's important to learn a foreign language."

Did you hear about the belt that went to prison?

It held up a pair of pants.

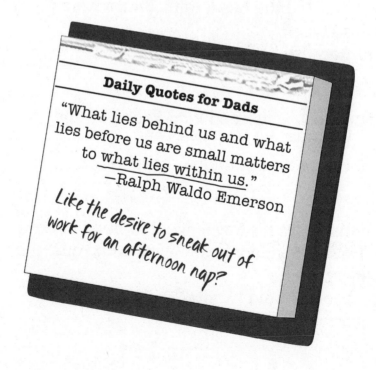

Daily Quotes for Dads

"What lies behind us and what lies before us are small matters to what lies within us."
—Ralph Waldo Emerson

Like the desire to sneak out of work for an afternoon nap?

You know you've resigned yourself to a dismal future when you catch yourself thinking, "My job might be soul-killing, but at least I've got a chair that spins!"

Q: Why did the raisin think things were going so well?
A: Because it was on a roll.

Q: Who will succeed King Rabbit on the throne?
A: Prince Bunny, the hare apparent.

A man calls his travel agent to book a flight. "How many people are flying with you?" the agent asks.

"How should I know?" he says. "I don't control the bookings."

Did you hear about the chiropractor who worked a double shift?
   He did it back to back.

Q: What did the janitor say when he jumped out of a closet?
A: "Supplies!"

@glenna_opt

we all had to sign a card for a coworker thats retiring and i just wrote "please take me with you" in it

Police officer: Sir, please open the door and come out immediately.
Me: But I'm going to the bathroom!
Police officer: Yes, but you're in a taxi!

On his deathbed, a businessman called his friend Bill. He said, "Bill…promise me that when I die, you'll have me cremated."

"Of course," Bill said. "What do you want me to do with your ashes?"

"Just put them in a box and mail them," the businessman replied, struggling for breath.

"Mail them?"

"To the IRS," he said weakly. "And write on the envelope, 'Now you have everything.'"

Mom: How's your class on Communist history going?
Teen: I had to drop out of it.
Mom: What for?
Teen: Lousy Marx.

A man tried to sell me a marionette for a shockingly low price. I should've known that there were strings attached.

Did you hear about the shiitake farmer? He worked hard, and eventually his business started to mushroom.

What dads say: "Wow, what a great story!"
What dads mean: "I tuned out 20 minutes ago because kids take forever to tell a story."

Dwight Eisenhower and Robert E. Lee
were leaders of men.
Generally speaking.

Q: What candy do sailors eat?
A: Lifesavers.

I got a letter from the bank saying that it
was a final notice. Great, they aren't going
to bug me anymore!

Q: How can you spot an anxious carpenter?
A: He bites his nails.

Two brothers named Hans and Sven were
walking by the fjord one day when Hans
fell in.
   Sven went home alone, and his mother
asked, "Sven, where is your brother?"
   "Look, Ma," he said, "no Hans."

"Let's stock up at the soil sale today," the landscaper said. "It's dirt cheap!"

Kid: Dad, I have practice after school. Can you bring my gym clothes?
Dad: No way! Tell Jim to bring his own clothes!

 @SkinnerSteven

HIPSTER COP: *into radio* "We've got a 13-88 in progress...it's a pretty rare crime, you probably wouldn't know it"

 @SkinnerSteven

Replying to @SkinnerSteven

HC: "in pursuit of suspect- on my vintage 1972 converted fixed gear varsity schwinn, of course"

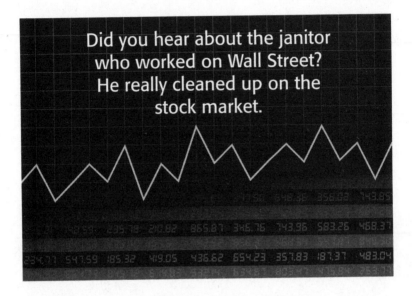

Did you hear about the janitor who worked on Wall Street? He really cleaned up on the stock market.

Q: What's the weirdest thing about a support group for hypochondriacs?

A: Members call in sick, but they all show up for the meeting anyway.

The other day, I was in an old building with an elevator run by a young operator. He kept calling me "son" even though I'm clearly older than him. "Why do you call me that?" I asked. He responded, "I brought you up, didn't I?"

Ideas that come off the top of your head
are hair-raising!

My dad worked for a hunting club that paid
him in venison and trophy heads. He was very
good at his job, which is why they paid him
the big bucks.

> **@Alllahdin**
> You can sit idle for days in your office
> but the moment you ask for a half day
> leave you become the strategically most
> important employee.
>
>

Never get into peach farming.
It's the pits!

YOU KNOW YOU'RE A DAD WHEN...

- you suddenly know all the words to every Eagles song.
- you get up early on a Saturday morning to make sure you'll be tired enough for a couch nap that afternoon.
- you change your car's oil exactly every 2,000 miles.
- mowing the lawn is no longer a chore, but a privilege.
- you can actually tell old John Wayne movies apart.
- your idea of fun is aimlessly wandering around the home improvement section of any store.

_____

Apparently, "Casual Friday" doesn't mean "show up in a ratty T-shirt and boxer shorts and eat chips all day at my desk."
They should've been more specific.

_____

Do you want to hear a joke about dairy farmers?
Never mind, it's too cheesy.

A man and his daughter got on a flight, and the stewardess directed the daughter to seat 2B.

"Oh, you got the Shakespeare seat," the dad said. "2B, get it?"

"Actually," the daughter said, "all seats are Shakespeare seats."

"How so?" the dad asked.

"They're all either 2B or not 2B."

I like to sleep with the lamp on.

My wife thinks it's weird, but I think it's cozy to sleep with something covering my head.

I vowed to be cool as a cucumber at work this week.

Unfortunately, I couldn't fit into that cool cucumber's tiny leather jacket and sunglasses.

BAD ADVICE FROM A REAL DAD

"'There's no future in those bloody computers, Son.' 35 years ago."

Q: What's a good name for a female firefighter?
A: Ashley.

As an electrician, I never have a hard time finding work. I'm just really good at making connections.

I went to school for a while to learn how to be a train driver. But then I got sidetracked.

A man gets hit by a car. As the paramedics load him into an ambulance, one of them asks, "Are you comfortable?"

"Oh, I make a good living," he replies.

Did you hear about the terrible singer who got locked out of his house?

He couldn't find his key.

A police officer stopped a man for driving the wrong way down a one-way street. "Where do you think you're going?" the cop asked.

"I'm not sure," the driver said, "but I must be late because everyone else is already going home."

 @AskThePankazzzz

We all have this colleague who, we hope, quits his job so everyone in the office is happy. If you don't know any such person, quit your job.

Did you hear about the scientist who cloned a deer?

She just used a doe-it-yourself kit.

I don't mind going to work. The true annoyance is having to stay there for 40 hours a week doing the jobs of four people while getting paid the salary of one.

The brain is a wonderful organ. It starts working the moment you get up in the morning, and does not stop until you get into the office.

—Robert Frost

A village blacksmith hired an apprentice. The blacksmith told the boy, "When I take the horseshoe out of the fire, I'll lay it on this anvil. And when I nod my head, you hit it with this hammer." The apprentice did just as he was told. And that's how *he* became the village blacksmith.

HUMOR IN THE HOUSE
Family Life and Creature Comforts

I want to be a billionaire, just like my dad.
He also wants to be a billionaire.

Q: What does a young computer call its father?
A: Data.

Kid: Dad, what does that sign say?
Dad: Nothing. You have to read it!

I get so annoyed when my wife reminds me to fix something. If I said I'm going to fix it, I'll fix it. There's no need to remind me about it every three months.

Q: Which breed of horse can jump higher than a house?
A: All breeds. Houses don't jump.

I spent $10,000 for a fancy new front door for the house.
I sure made a grand entrance.

Knock-knock!
Who's there?
Honeydew.
Honeydew who?
Honeydew you know how fine you look right now? It's too bad we cantaloupe.

I intended to buy eight cans of Sprite.
But when I got home, I realized I'd picked seven up.

Kid: Why do you stand on one leg while you get money out of the ATM?
Dad: I'm checking my balance.

After dinner, my wife asked if I could clear the table. I needed a running start, but I made it over!

Q: What kind of dog swims the best?
A: A lap dog.

I had a good dad.
Or at least he was a better dad
than his jokes were.

_____

Q: What's the favorite color of a dad who's answering the phone?
A: "Yellow!"

@simoncholland

I'm at my most hostage negotiator when I see my 3 year old holding a permanent marker without the lid.

The best part of the movie is whatever part you missed when you had to take your kid to the bathroom.

_____

Kid: My math teacher said I'm average.
Parent: Well, that's just mean.

My mother: You have a piece of glitter on your face.
Me: Oh, Bobby did an art project at school that had glitter.
My mother: Cute! Let me see!
Me: It was three years ago.

I thought your mom's wedding ring was expensive. Think of how much Saturn's must have cost.

LIES DADS TELL

"I don't have a favorite child."

"I definitely can tell that this is a drawing of a cow."

"I certainly ate my vegetables when I was your age!"

A wife was making fried eggs for breakfast. Suddenly, her husband burst into the kitchen. "Careful," he said. "*Careful!* Add some more butter! My gosh! You're cooking too many at once. *Too many!* Turn them! *Turn them now!* We need more butter. Oh, dear! They're going to *stick*! Careful. I said be *careful*! You *never* listen to me when you're cooking! Never! Turn them! Hurry! Are you *crazy*? Have you lost your mind? Don't forget to salt them. You know you always forget to salt them. Use the salt. *Use the salt!*"

The wife glared at her husband. "What in the world is wrong with you? You think I don't know how to fry some eggs?"

The husband replied, "I just wanted to show you what it feels like when I'm driving."

I've had five children.
I'm kidding!

Dad: Today in the park I pet a gosling!
Child: Really?
Dad: Yep. I was feeling a little down.

You know what they say about
really smart kids.
They're often in a class by themselves.

Knock-knock!
Who's there?
Amazon.
Amazon who?
Amazon of my mother and father.

I told my wife I was afraid I took too many
sleeping pills. She advised me to have a
few drinks and get some rest.

A guy spots a sign outside a house that reads "Talking Dog for Sale." Intrigued, he knocks on the door and inquires about the dog. The dog's owner whistles and calls, "Harry!"

Harry the dog runs over. "So," the prospective buyer says to the dog, "what kind of life have you led?"

"A very full one," Harry responds. "I lived in the Alps, where I rescued avalanche victims. Then I served my country in Afghanistan. Now I spend my days lecturing at schools and reading to nursing home residents."

The guy can't believe it. He asks the owner, "Why would you want to sell this incredible dog?"

The owner says, "Because he's a liar! He never did half those things!"

Did you hear about the lemon that got suspended from school? It was constantly tarty.

Fun prank to play on your kids:
Empty a small bag of Cheetos, refill it with baby carrots, and glue it shut. Snack on Cheetos while you wait for them to notice.

A giant dinosaur terrorized my city! It threatened "to annihilate the city, to destroy, to demolish, to obliterate, to ravage, to ruin..."

As it went on, I realized it was the most terrifying species of all: a Tyrannothesaurus rex.

Q: Which side of a horse has more hair?
A: The outside.

My girlfriend called me lazy the other day. Can you believe she woke me up at 3 p.m. to tell me that?

A college professor hands her student a book by her favorite motivational speaker. "You should read this," she says.

"Oh, I've read all of his books," the student replies. "I should probably return them before he notices they're missing."

I studied abroad in college.
And then I asked her to marry me.

Nanny: Now, can you tell me what comes after S in the alphabet?
Kid: T!
Nanny: Great, I'll have mine with milk and sugar. Thanks!

Grapes are no good these days.
You know what the problem is?
People aren't raisin them right.

Son: Some kid just came up and dumped milk on my shoes and threw cheese at me!
Dad: How dairy!

Q: What's the one thing that Adam and Eve didn't have in the Garden of Eden that everybody since then has had?
A: Parents.

A girl met a horse, and they became fast friends. The horse ended up moving around a lot, though, and they lost touch.
　　It turns out he was unstable.

Child: Where do spoons come from?
Father: The spork.

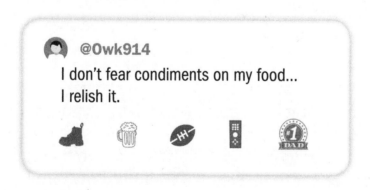

> **@Owk914**
> I don't fear condiments on my food...
> I relish it.

The almond and the pea fell in love and had a baby. They named her Peanut.

Q: How do locomotives get from point A to point B?
A: Lots of training.

A police officer pulls over a car to the side of the road. The officer asks the driver, "How long have you been driving without a taillight?"

The man hollers, "Oh no!" and jumps out of the car to inspect it. "Wait until my family finds out about this!"

"And where is your family?" the officer asks.

"Er," the man says, "they were in the trailer that was hitched up to the back of the car!"

Kid: Can I leave the table?
Dad: Where are you going to leave it?

With one arm full of stuff, my wife tried to unlatch our baby's car seat with the other hand. In the middle of her struggle, she wondered out loud, "How do people with one arm do this?"

I replied, "Single-handedly."

 @outsmartedmommy

I never knew you could do a job that you pretended to know what you were doing for longer than 3 years until I became a parent.

My dad asked me to mail out the invitations to my brother's surprise birthday party.

And that's when I realized that my brother was his favorite twin.

Son: What does *bargain* mean?
Dad: Well, it means a great deal, actually…

A vowel saves another vowel's life.
The other vowel thanks him, saying,
"Aye E! I owe you!"

Great Moments in Dad History

July 9, 1953. George Kinsley becomes the first dad to angrily shut a door left open for five seconds while yelling, "I'm not paying to air-condition the whole neighborhood!"

Q: Why do dads tell dad jokes?
A: Because grandpa jokes fell asleep on the couch.

Kid: Can you put my shoes on?
Uncle: No, I don't think they'll fit me.

During a business trip, a man passed through the college town where his son Jimmy went to school. Deciding to surprise his son with dinner, he drove to the fraternity house where Jimmy lived. He knocked on the door, but nobody answered. Hearing loud music inside, he knocked louder. Finally, he banged on the door until somebody stuck his head out of a window on the second floor. "Hey, what is it?" the guy shouted down.

"Does Jimmy Robertson live here?" the father asked.

"Yeah," the guy said. "Just leave him on the porch, and we'll grab him in the morning."

My grandpa named his dogs Timex, Rolex, and Swatch.
Those are his watch dogs.

Q: How many dads does it take to kill a spider?
A: One.

Daughter: Good night, Daddy!
Dad: It is now!

A turtle was crossing the road when he was mugged by two snails. Once the police showed up, they asked him to explain what happened. The turtle replied, "I don't know. It all happened so fast!"

Did you hear about the princess who started a bakery?

It rose to success, as she was quite well-bread.

Mom: Do you need a pocket calculator for school?
Son: No, I know exactly how many pockets I've got.

A family was at an amusement park. When the young daughter got tired, her dad put her up on his shoulders. But then she started picking at his hair. Wincing, her dad said, "If you keep pulling my hair, you're going to have to get down off my shoulders."

"But Dad," the kid replied, "I'm just trying to get my gum back."

BAD ADVICE FROM A REAL DAD

"My dad (who has a bachelor's degree in finance) told me that you can use credit cards as free money as long as you pay the minimum payments."

Who cares if I don't know what *apocalypse* means?
It's not the end of the world.

Mother: Be yourself and don't do anything stupid.
Teenager: So…which one then?

Communism jokes aren't funny.
Unless everyone gets them.

Q: How can you tell if a parrot has been in your fridge?
A: The butter is covered in colorful feathers.

During a fancy dinner party, the two children of the hosts tiptoe into the dining room, completely naked. They walk slowly around the table, giggling quietly. Embarrassed, their parents act like nothing out of the ordinary is happening, and they try to keep the dinner conversation going. Following their lead, the guests do the same. After the kids walk around the table a few times, there's an awkward silence, during which one of the kids says, "See, I told you. It *is* vanishing cream!"

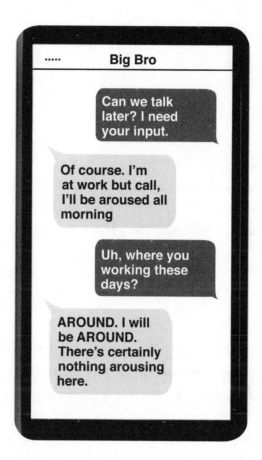

Girlfriend: I like your pajamas. Are they satin?
Boyfriend: Nope, not worn. Brand new!

If it ain't broke, well, the kids
haven't gotten ahold of it yet.

Son: Was I adopted?
Parent: Not yet, but we're still holding out hope.

 @daddydoinwork

My kid just flushed her socks down the toilet because "dirty stuff goes there." Sound logic, questionable execution.

A horse moved in next door. I hope he has a stable income. I should go say, "Hay, welcome to the neigh-borhood!"

Knock-knock!
Who's there?
Ralph.
Ralph who?
Ralph! Ralph! I'm a dog!

What dads say: "Ask your mother."
What dads mean: "No, but I don't want to be the bad guy."

There are times when parenthood seems nothing more than feeding the hand that bites you.

—Peter De Vries

I did that "airplane" trick to get my toddler to eat some food.

Now all he wants to eat are airplanes. It's costing me a fortune.

Parent: Why did you get such a bad score on this test?
Kid: Absence.
Parent: What? You were at school that day.
Kid: Yeah, but the smart kid I sit next to wasn't.

I had to look up the definition of *opaque*.
But it wasn't very clear.

Q: What's a good name for a hot dog?
A: Frank.

Q: What's a good name for a hot dog truck?
A: Frank Truck.

Johnny was in the garden filling in a hole with dirt when his neighbor peered over the fence. "What are you up to, Johnny?" the neighbor asked.

"My goldfish died," replied Johnny. "I just buried him."

The neighbor saw the big mound of dirt and remarked, "That's an awfully big hole for a goldfish."

Johnny patted down the last heap of dirt and replied, "That's because he's inside your cat."

Kid: Dad, name two pronouns.
Dad: Who, me?

Knock-knock!
Who's there?
Tyrone.
Tyrone who?
Tyrone shoelaces!

The circle is such a
ridiculous shape.
There's just no
point to it.

Kid: Dad, why is my name Churchill?
Dad: Your mom wanted to name you after
someone she admired.
Other Kid: What about me?
Dad: I got to name you, for the same reason.
Now, off to bed, Limp Bizkit.

Q: Why do dramatic teenagers hang out in groups of 3, 5, or 7?
A: Because they can't even.

A boy gets in trouble for not listening to his mother and is sent to his room. After a few minutes, the father goes in. "Do you know why you're in trouble? You disobeyed your mom," the dad says. "And if *I'm* not allowed to do that, then you certainly aren't!"

You should learn sign language.
It's very handy.

Before I got married, I had six theories about raising children; now, I have six children and no theories.
—John Wilmot

Nothing lasts forever.
Except for my kid's baseball games.

 You can tell it's the day your child graduates from high school because that's the day you finally install her car seat correctly.

My family ran a major fishing business. Anybody in the area who wanted to catch or sell any fish had to get permission from Grandpa. That's why they called him the Cod Father.

Q: Where will you find the inside scoop?
A: In the kitchen drawer.

"How did the car wind up in the living room?" the angry father asks his teenager as they survey the massive damage to the house.
   "Simply put," the boy replies, "I took a left at the kitchen."

When I got married, my mother told me to always remember that marriage is hard. Especially for the person who's married to me.

Her: I'm trying on this new dress—can you zip it?
Him (after a long pause): Hey, what did I say wrong, anyway?

Knock-knock!
Who's there?
Russell.
Russell who?
Let's Russell up some grub!

Sister: Hey, check out my new pen.
Brother: What's so great about it?
Sister: It can write underwater.
Brother: Can it write other words, too?

Q: What makes a kid laugh hardest at your dad jokes?
A: When she needs 20 bucks.

A man was busy at work one day when he received a call. "This is the school calling about your son, Darren," a woman said. "He's been caught telling wild lies."

"Indeed!" the man said. "I don't have a son."

Great Moments in Dad History

June 29, 1984: Carl Smith is the first dad to leave a message on his daughter's answering machine, identifying himself by his first and last name as well as "your father."

Q: How is dinnertime like medieval times?
A: The amount of planning and trickery it takes to sneak anything remotely healthy into a child's meal is basically what it took to poison a wicked medieval king.

Q: What sound does a 6 a.m. Saturday alarm clock make?
A: "Daaaaaaaaaaad!"

One day, a dad hears a knock at the door. An older man is standing on his porch. "I'm so sorry," the visitor says, "but I think I've run over your cat. I'd like to replace him."

"Okay," the dad says, "but how good are you at catching mice?"

Customer: I bought this sweater for my grandfather the other day, but it's picking up a lot of static electricity.
Clerk: Sorry, sir, we'll replace it. Free of charge.

Public service announcement for kids:
"It's time to go to bed" is a statement of fact, not the first stage in a negotiation process.

My girlfriend is leaving me. She says I'm too obsessed with science fiction. What alternate universe is *she* living in?

Q: What's the worst thing somebody can do to your kid?
A: Give him a whistle.

For his birthday, a boy wants a pet spider. His dad takes him to an exotic pet store, where they see a big, hairy spider. The father asks how much it costs. "That's fifty dollars," the clerk replies.

"Fifty bucks!" the dad exclaims. "Forget that, I'll just find a cheap one off the web."

Mom: This is the last straw!
Dad: We'll buy more.

It is my solemn duty as a dad to make sure those cookies taste all right and are not poisoned. You know, for the family.

"We can't clean the house right now," the husband reasoned. "If we did that, we'd have nothing to do during spring cleaning time."

My aunt was caught shoplifting a turkey from a supermarket. As she headed out the door, a security guard stopped her and said, "Hey, what do you think you're doing with that turkey?"

She replied, "Probably some mashed potatoes, stuffing, and a green bean casserole."

Knock-knock!
Who's there?
Taylor.
Taylor who?
Taylor little brother to pick up his toys so I don't step on them.

Kid: What if I fall off my bike and hurt myself?
Mom: Well, I'd call you a doctor!
Dad: Now, how is that going to help him? He's sitting there with a broken arm, and you're shouting, "You're a doctor!"?

I always carry a picture of my family in my wallet. It's a reminder of why there's no money in my wallet.

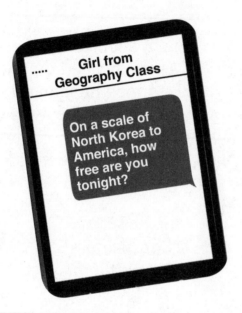

One afternoon, a teenager hears the doorbell ring. Standing on the porch is a man who's disheveled and angry. "Your dog jumped your fence, chased me on a bicycle, tackled me, and bit my leg!" the man yells.

The teen looks the visitor up and down, glances at his dog in the yard, and says, "That's impossible. My dog doesn't know how to ride a bicycle."

Dad: What're you up to?
Son: Just thinking.
Dad: Ah, that must be what I smelled burning.

I tried to ask my wife an important question the other day. But she was applying a mud facial treatment.

You should have seen the dirty look she gave me.

Daily Quotes for Dads

"Kids are hilarious...They don't really know what they're saying, and that just makes much more funniness happen."
—Kenan Thompson

Unless they tell Mom about the candy for breakfast—then the fun ends.

Children left alone in the back seat of a car can cause accidents. That's pretty ironic, considering that accidents in the back seat of a car can lead to children.

Q: Why did the teenaged bird go to the beach?
A: He heard there were going to be gulls there.

A mother pounded on her son's bedroom door one morning. "Get up! You're going to be late for school!" she yelled.

A voice inside the room called back, "I'm not going. Everybody there hates me, and I hate it, and you can't make me go!"

"Listen," his mother said. "I'll give you two reasons why you have to. First, you're 40 years old. Second, you're the principal."

Kid: Hey, Dad, are you all right?
Dad: Nope, I'm half left.

No matter how kind you may be,
remember that German kids are kinder.

What dads say: "It's past your bedtime."
What dads mean: "Daddy and Mommy need
some 'alone time.'"

Knock-knock!
Who's there?
Amanda.
Amanda who?
Amanda fix the toilet!

I went to a cable TV repairman's wedding
last weekend.
The reception was fantastic.

Q: Why should you buy a dog when your kids
become teenagers?
A: So you have someone who's happy to see
you when you come home.

Wife: Honey, you should write a book about your life.
Husband: Now *that's* a novel idea!

___

At the grocery store, a man is looking for a large enough Thanksgiving turkey to feed his family, but he can't find one to his liking. "Do these turkeys get any bigger?" he asks an employee.
　　She replies, "No, sir, they've stopped growing. These turkeys are dead, you see."

Great Moments in Dad History

October 4, 1971: Upon dropping off his child at a friend's house for the fourth day in a row, a dad named Ted Barnes bellows for the first time, "I'm not running a taxi service here!"

My wife and I met when we were both gymnasts. I was doing a backflip one day when I realized I was heels over head in love.

Dad: What are you making for dinner?
Mom: Venison.
Dad: Oh, deer!

I was so relieved when my son was born.
It looked like he was running out of
womb in there.

Q: How many kids does it take to change the toilet paper roll?
A: Who knows? No kid has ever done it.

Just before Christmas, a child's behavior is usually affected by the laws of Claus-and-effect.

A couple sits on the porch, watching the sunset, each with a beer in hand. The husband says, "I love you so much."

The wife says, "I love you, too. But is that you or the beer talking?"

The husband answers, "It's me, talking to my beer."

Dad: What are you doing to that wall?
College student: Drilling holes to hang things.
Dad: Sounds boring.

Real men wear pink.
At least they do if that's the color of the shirt their wife just bought them.

Q: Why did the cowboy buy a wiener dog?
A: Because someone told him to get a long, little doggie.

Knock-knock!
Who's there?
Linda.
Linda who?
Linda hand, I can't move this piano by myself!

 @daddysdigest

Wife: She's wearing her princess dress. Pretend you're her servant.

Me: Pretend?

Back when I was a kid, I had a rare disease. In order to survive, I had to eat dirt three times a day.

I'm so glad my older brother told me I had it!

Mom: Do you know where the English Channel is?
Son: I'm not sure, ever since we switched cable companies last week.

―――――――

If you've ever tried to nail grape jelly to the ceiling, then you'll understand what it's like trying to raise teenagers.

―――――――

I love being married. I was single for a long time, and I just got so sick of finishing my own sentences.
―Brian Kiley

―――――――

Q: What's a good name for a guy who can never remember where he parked his car?
A: Carlos.

―――――――

My family went out for the afternoon, so I decided to cook them dinner as a special treat. But when they came home, the fire trucks ruined the surprise.

A hungover man stumbles into the kitchen one morning.

"I'm guessing you feel terrible," his wife remarks, sipping her tea.

"Actually, I feel okay," he says, pouring himself some coffee. "I slept like a log."

"You didn't even come to bed!"

"I know," he says. "I passed out in the fireplace."

Knock-knock!
Who's there?
Raymond.
Raymond who?
Raymond me to go to the store—
we're out of milk.

Kid: Dad, what's the difference between one yard and two yards?
Dad: A fence.

A middle school kid comes home, goes straight to his room, and flops down on his bed in defeat.

His dad follows him. "Hey, bud, how did the test go?" he asks.

"Well," the son says, his words muffled, "I did what George Washington did."

"What's that?" the father asks.

The son answers, "I went down in history."

Do I want to go to a haunted cornfield maze? Heavens, no! If I wanted to get trapped in a disorienting maze, I'd just walk into my kid's bedroom.

People who celebrate Christmas experience four stages of life:

Stage 1. You believe in Santa Claus.

Stage 2. You stop believing in Santa Claus.

Stage 3. You are Santa Claus.

Stage 4. You look like Santa Claus.

Child: Dad, why are you sleeping on the chandelier?
Dad: I'm a light sleeper.

A couple of guys are arguing about which one of them has the smarter dog. "Mine is so smart," the first guy says, "that every morning he brings the newspaper to me along with scrambled eggs and a fresh cup of hot coffee."

"Oh, I know," says the other guy. "My dog told me all about it."

Knock-knock!
Who's there?
Cynthia.
Cynthia who?
Cynthia been so good,
I'm taking you out for pizza!

@AndrewKirk6

Being a parent is basically walking around your housing playing the game "Is that chocolate, poop, or dirt?" And never winning.

Fun prank to play on your kid:
When she asks if she can sleep in your bed, say yes, and then slip on a clown mask.

My wife: Can I be frank?
Me: Sure, but we're going to have to go down to city hall to get the name change forms.

Q: How do you make antifreeze?
A: Steal her snow pants while they're drying by the fire.

Q: What's the loneliest cheese?
A: Provolone.

A kid sees his grandfather working in the garden and goes out to join him. "What do you put on your celery?" the grandson asks.

The grandpa stops digging for a second, touched by his grandson's interest. "Well," he says, "usually a mix of bonemeal-enriched soil, fertilizer, and a little horse manure."

"Gross!" the grandson says. "I just use peanut butter."

The best way to remember your wife's birthday is to forget it once.

—E. Joseph Cossman

What dads say: "Maybe."
What dads mean: "No."

90 percent of parenting is...
- Watching when someone says "watch this!"
- Pretending to be asleep.
- Shuttling kids to and from public bathrooms.
- Letting kids play games on your phone.
- Being late for things.
- Collecting box tops.
- Filling out permission slips.

The other 10 percent is...
- Heartwarming moments you share with your children that make it all worthwhile.
- Drinking beer in the garage after they go to bed.

My daughter thinks we don't give her enough privacy. Can you believe she wrote that in her diary?

Wife: Hey, I thought you were going to mow the lawn today.
Husband: I *am* mowing the lawn.
Wife: No, you're not. You're goofing off.
Husband: No, I'm just taking a break. Well, several breaks. In a row.

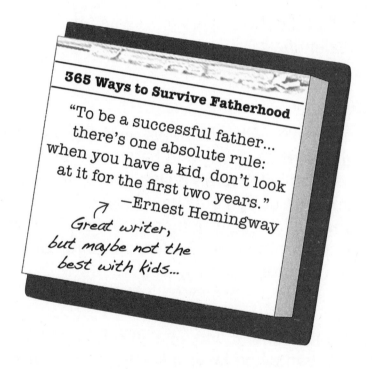

365 Ways to Survive Fatherhood

"To be a successful father... there's one absolute rule: when you have a kid, don't look at it for the first two years."
—Ernest Hemingway

Great writer, but maybe not the best with kids...

My kids wonder why I watch the same Bruce Willis movie every day.
But hey, old habits *Die Hard*.

Knock-knock!
Who's there?
Emily.
Emily who?
I have no idea. My name is Dave.

Q: What did the chef give his wife for Valentine's Day?
A: Hugs and quiches.

A dad pulls aside one of his twin sons at their eighth birthday party and hands the boy a five-dollar bill. "Here's a little something extra from me. But don't tell your brother."

The kid looks at the money and says, "Sorry, if you want me to stay quiet, it's going to cost you a lot more than five bucks."

Since I became a dad, I get into trouble more often than when I was a kid. It's mostly when my kids get scolded by their mother for doing something wrong, and they protest, "But Dad does it all the time!"

Dad: Do you know why cartoon ducks wear pants?
Son: No, why?
Dad: Otherwise everyone would see their quacks.

Our dog doesn't really like swimming, but he likes to hang out in the lake and float. He's a very good buoy.

My wife was beating herself up over something she did wrong the other day, but I told her she should just embrace her mistakes. She agreed.
Then she gave me a big hug!

Q: What do farmers give their wives on Valentine's Day?
A: Hogs and kisses.

The other day, a German shepherd peed on my front lawn, right in front of me. And today, he brought his dog with him.

When I die, my son stands to inherit my bathroom scale. Where there's a will, there's a weigh.

A married couple was discussing their final wishes, burial plans, and things of that nature. "I want you to know that I don't want to live in a vegetative state," the husband said. "Being hooked up to machines is no way to live. If that ever happens, just pull the plug."

Silently, the woman stood up and unplugged his laptop and the family's video game console. Then she grabbed her husband's phone and threw it as hard as she could at the TV, shattering both.

I just bought a book called
How to Avoid Scams.
Best $500 I ever spent!

 @simoncholland

Today my 4 year old was so tired she
could barely keep her eyes open. Then
she slept for 86 seconds in the car and
will now be up forever.

When I turned 18, I bought a locket
and put my own picture in it.
I just wanted to be independent.

Knock-knock!
Who's there?
Colleen.
Colleen who?
Colleen up this mess out here!

Kid: I saw a deer on the way to school today.
Dad: Neat! But how did you know it was on its way to school?

I was supposed to meet my date at the gym, but she didn't show up.
I guess we're not going to work out.

Q: What's the difference between pizza and pizza jokes?
A: Pizza jokes can't be topped!

Q: Who is bigger, Ms. Bigger or her baby?
A: The baby. She's a little Bigger.

"Marriage is not just spiritual communion, it is also remembering to take out the trash."

—Dr. Joyce Brothers

A nut enrolled in the University of Hawaii. It was interested in pursuing higher macademia.

Q: Which farm animal is a cannibal?
A: A cow. It eats its fodder.

Q: What hotel did the cheese stay in?
A: The Stilton.

Knock-knock!
Who's there?
Icing.
Icing who?
Icing really loud.

Sometimes I'll open a root beer and it fizzes so loudly that it sounds like it's talking to me. You know, soda speak.

Q: Why do cowboys put big hats and boots on their salads?
A: They prefer ranch dressing.

When asked how Swiss cheese is made, the dad said, "From hole milk."

Q: Which is more useful, the Sun or the Moon?
A: The Moon, because the Sun only shines in the daytime. And it's light then anyway.

Every Saturday, a dad and his kids played Cops and Robbers. They ran around the house, chasing each other with toy guns. One day, one of the kids cornered the dad and "shot" him. He slumped to the ground, giving a dramatic death scene before lying totally motionless. As they pounced on him, he continued to lie there without moving a muscle…for 10 minutes.

The kids got scared and went to get their mother. "Honey, are you okay?" she asked her husband, jostling him by the shoulder.

"Quiet!" he whispered. "This is the only chance I get to take a nap around here."

Q: How do you stop a dog from barking in the back of the car?
A: Move him up to the front seat.

 @DadandBuried

It's when my son yells at me that "the blueberries go IN the waffles, not ON the waffles!" that I realize he's not paying me nearly enough.

Kid: Dad, can you just do my homework for me?
Dad: Of course not. It wouldn't be right.
Kid: You could try, though.

_____

They say that the better a man smells, the more he enjoys Valentine's Day.
It turns out that men are scent-imental.

My daughter brought me breakfast in bed today—scrambled eggs. They weren't all they were cracked up to be.

Brother: I bet I can guess what's in this present.
Sister: Really?
Brother: Yep. It's a gift.

I think my wife has been adding extra soil to the garden.
The plot thickens!

Did you hear about the drummer whose girlfriend gave birth to twin daughters?
He named them Anna 1, Anna 2.

Kid: Want to play a game of checkers?
Dad: Sure, but I'm the Arnold Schwarzenegger of checkers.
Kid: What does that mean?
Dad: I'll be black!

A dad pushed a tack into the wall. Standing below it, he called, "Hey, kids, c'mere!" When they gathered, he cried out, "Help me, I'm under a tack!"

My dog loves going down to the pond, but we can't take him anymore because the ducks always attack him.

I guess I shouldn't have bought a pure bread dog.

Q: How do you get a lady from a farm to like you?
A: Just a tractor.

A kid presented her father with a drawing of Earth that she made in school. "Do you like it, Daddy?" she asked.

"Sweetie," he said, "this means the world to me."

My wife bought me a brown leather jacket. I thought it was extremely ugly, yet I wore it anyway.

I'm easily suede.

 @WoodyLuvsCoffee
Movie tickets for 4: $56
Popcorn: $16
Hot dogs: $20
Sodas: $14
Candy: $15
Parking: $5
Seeing the smiles on your family's faces: $126

Husband: Remind me to call the doctor today.
Wife: Which doctor?
Husband: No, just a regular one.

Did you hear about the guy whose partner hogged all the blankets while they were sleeping?

Don't worry, he recovered.

_____

What dads say: "Can anyone recommend some math and science books my kid can study over the summer?"
What dads mean: "My kid is a freaking genius, and I'm bragging."

_____

A boy came bounding down the stairs with a loud stomp-stomp-stomp. Annoyed, his father bellowed, "Son! How many times have I told you not to run down those stairs?" Turning the kid around, he said, "I want you to go back up, and then come down much quieter." The boy did as he was told and headed back upstairs.

A few minutes passed, and the doorbell rang. The dad answered the door, and there stood the son, who said, "I took the window."

Little girl: Uh-oh, the cat threw up on the carpet!
Parent: He must not be feline well.

Q: Why did the rhyme-reciting chicken cross the road?
A: It was poultry in motion.

Q: Why did the cow cross the road?
A: Because it wasn't chicken.

Knock-knock!
Who's there?
Guitar.
Guitar who?
Guitar coats, it's time to go.

Boyfriend: Did you hear the joke about the dirty gym socks?
Girlfriend: I did. It stinks!

Q: What do baby bears eat?
A: Cub sandwiches.

We got our daughter a minifridge for her room.
I can't wait to see her face light up when she opens it!

Boy: There's a hole in your shoe.
Younger sibling: No, there isn't!
Boy: Then how did you get your foot into it?

Two silkworms had a race, but they ultimately ended in a tie.

Q: Why did the piece of coal turn into a diamond?
A: It just couldn't take the pressure.

Did you know that dragons are nocturnal animals?
They sleep all day so they can fight knights.

Kid: Ew, there's a bunch of ants on my chocolate bar!
Dad: Aha, so there *is* life on Mars!

Teacher: Your kid is such a free spirit! Don't you just love that?
Me: If by "free spirits" you mean an open bar, then yes, I love it.

Q: How does a dog stop a movie?
A: She presses paws.

Falling down a stairwell is easy.
You just take it step by step.

Wife: Hon, you dropped some ice cubes… Wait, don't just kick them under the refrigerator!
Husband: Whatever. Now it's all just water under the fridge.

Q: How do you make your waterbed bouncier?
A: Use spring water.

Kid: Dad, what's an anagram for *nuclear*?
Dad: That's unclear.

"Honesty is the best policy."
That's according to dad aka the Easter Bunny, Santa Claus, and the Tooth Fairy.

Did you hear about the dad who sliced his fingers while cutting cheese?
It was indicative of grater problems.

I think my experience as a goat farmer will prepare me well for fatherhood.
I'm great around kids!

Dad: When you grow up, marry someone who tends to bees.
Daughter: Why, Dad?
Dad: Because they're a keeper.

Q: What's the difference between Ferdinand Magellan and plastic wrap?
A: One is a discoverer, and the other is a dish coverer.

Every time I see a "Keep Off the Grass" sign, I wonder how did it get there in the first place?

Teen: Dad, I'm trying to FaceTime my friends. Did you rub Vaseline all over the camera lens on my phone?
Dad: Yep!
Teen: Why?
Dad: Now you've been photo-balmed!

Knock-knock!
Who's—?
The dad inside hisses, "Pretend we're not home! I don't want to buy anything."

I like telling dad jokes.
And sometimes he even laughs!

SPORTS AND LEISURE
aka What Dads Don't Have Time For

@MrGirlDad

A journey of a thousand miles begins with a single step...immediately followed by a dropped pacifier and a thousand miles of screaming.

Knock-knock!
Who's there?
A magically refilling glass of beer.
Well, come on in!

Q: What do you call a bunch of dads hanging out together?
A: A pa-ty.

Q: How do you peer-pressure a hipster?
A: "C'mon, man, no one else is doing it!"

A 13-year-old boy and his father were listening to music on the car radio. The boy asked, "Dad, what kind of music did you listen to when you were my age?"

"Oh, I was a big fan of the Beatles," the father replied.

"The who?"

"Oh, sure," the dad said. "I liked them, too."

Why is it that one match can start a forest fire, but it takes a whole box to light a barbecue?

A guy goes ice fishing for the first time. While waiting for a bite, he hears a mysterious, booming voice say, "There are no fish under the ice!" The man ignores it, moves spots, cuts a hole, and starts fishing again. Once more, the voice says, "There are no fish under the ice!"

He looks up and says, "Lord?"

"No," the voice says. "I'm the ice rink manager!"

I take my B vitamin every day.
By which I mean Bud Lite.

Wife: What's this movie about?

Husband: Oh, two hours or so.

A furniture store keeps calling me, even though I never call back.
All I wanted was one night stand.

Q: What kind of sandwich does an opera singer eat?
A: Sol-La-Miiiiii!

A slice of apple pie is $2.50 in Jamaica and $3.00 in the Bahamas.
These are the pie rates of the Caribbean.

Q: What instrument is Monica afraid of?
A: A harmonica.

Q: In what language are stomach rumbles?
A: Hungarian.

First rule of
Procrastination Club:
I'll tell you tomorrow.

Three soldiers in
training headed into
town and got too
drunk at a bar.
They knew they
were off base.

Q: How does Dracula
play baseball?
A: With a vampire bat.

Q: What do you wear
to Jurassic Park?
A: A Jurassic parka.

Golfer:
Notice any
improvement
since last
year?
Caddie:
Polished
your clubs,
did you?

Knock-knock!
Who's there?
Orson.
Orson who?
Stop Orson around!

 A few decades ago, no one would've guessed that half of our time away from the house would be spent hunched over a power outlet trying to juice up enough to play *Candy Crush*.

I'm so good at sleeping, I can do it with my eyes closed!

There should be a children's song: 'If You're Happy and You Know It, Keep it to Yourself and Let Your Dad Sleep.'

—Jim Gaffigan

Q: How does Darth Vader like his toast?
A: On the dark side.

I don't play hacky sack to look cool.
I do it just for kicks.

Q: What's the difference between a poorly-dressed man on a bicycle and a well-dressed man on a unicycle?
A: Attire.

Great Moments in Dad History

June 28, 1972: With his noisy kids fighting in the back seat, Grant Golden becomes the first dad to threaten to turn his station wagon around and cancel their trip to Disney World.
(He doesn't follow through with it.)

Interviewer: Can you perform under pressure?
Applicant: No, but I can do a pretty good "Bohemian Rhapsody."

Seth always looked on the bright side. No matter how horrible the circumstances, he would always say, "Eh, it could have been worse." In fact, his outlook was so incessantly optimistic that it irritated his friends.

One day, Seth went golfing with his buddies. They were eager to tell him a story so awful that even Seth couldn't put a positive spin on it. While teeing up, one of them said, "Seth, did you hear about Tom? He came home last night, found his wife in bed with another man, and shot the guy!"

"That's awful!" said Seth. "But it could have been worse."

"How could it have been worse than that?"

"Well," replied Seth, "if it had happened the night before, I'd be dead now!"

A woman hands her husband two kayak paddles. "Which one do you want?" she asks.

He replies, "Either oar."

Q: Why can't DJs play billiards?
A: They always scratch.

I've never gone to a gun range before.
Today, I decided to give it a shot!

 @TimothyAlex

Parenting your kids is most rewarding
when they're napping and you are
napping too.

First guy: How good is your dad at golf?
Second guy: He's tee-riffic.

I love astronomy.
The rotation of Earth really makes my day.

Basketball players are always so well-rested.
You see, taller people sleep longer.

Did you hear about the basketball
player who went to jail?
He shot the ball.

Q: Why do you never see hippos hiding in
trees?
A: Because they're very good at it.

Did you hear about the panda's
birthday party?
It was total pandemonium.

Knock-knock!
Who's there?
Hewlett.
Hewlett who?
Hewlett the dogs out?!

A lonely bachelor wants company, so he buys a pet centipede and a little wooden box for it to live in. Later that day, he decides to go out. "Want to go get a bite to eat?" he asks the centipede. There's no answer. A minute later, he asks again. Again, no reply. Finally, he shouts, "Hey! Do you want to go out to dinner?"

He hears a small, annoyed voice say, "Hold your horses! I'm putting on my shoes!"

@robwhisman

sick of these pseudo "hipsters" in their abercrombie & fitch shirts who probly can't even name one abercrombie & fitch album

Do you know the story about the chicken that ran across the freeway and crossed the border?

Me neither. I couldn't follow it.

A muscular 6'5", 275-pound college freshman decided to try out for his school's football team. "Can you tackle?" the coach asked. Immediately, the freshman ran over to a telephone pole and knocked it over, breaking it into splinters. Impressed, the coach asked, "Can you run?" Before the coach could get out his stopwatch, the freshman had run all the way down the field and back. "Wow!" the coach exclaimed. "But can you pass a football?"

The freshman thought for a moment and answered, "Probably, Coach. If I can swallow the ball, I bet I could pass it."

Never buy anything made with Velcro.
It's a total rip-off!

Q: Where do tiger cubs learn to swim?
A: In the kitty pool.

Did you know that milk is the fastest liquid on earth?
Yeah, it's pasteurized before you even see it.

Customer at Chinese restaurant: Is your soup heavy or light?
Waiter: Heavy. It's one ton.

Q: What do you get when you mix wine with gasoline?
A: Vin Diesel.

Can't wait to take my sweet new ride for a spin! Comes equipped with cell phone holder, cupholder, and luggage rack, and tops out at 6 mph.

Did you hear about the movie version of *Merriam-Webster Dictionary*?
It was a defining moment in cinema.

Kid: What's on TV?
Dad: Dust.

Q: Where do quarterbacks keep notes on their passes?
A: In a spiral notebook.

I applied to Hogwarts School of Witchcraft and Wizardry but never got a response, as it apparently doesn't exist.
Guess I'm going to have to go fight in the Star Wars instead.

 @thenatewolf

Me: goodnight kids

Kids: goodnight dad

Me: goodnight monster that eats children who are bad

Wife: [through radio under the bed] GOODNIGHT

Q: What do French cows say?
A: "Moo la la!"

Q: Why was Samuel Morse a terrible poker player?
A: He always telegraphed his hand.

I told the cops they couldn't come in my house without a warrant. So they started singing "Cherry Pie," came in, and arrested me.

I'm allergic to grass. Hey, it could be worse. I could be allergic to beer.

—Greg Norman

Q: What doughnut can you smoke?
A: A cream puff.

Dad: What do you want for dessert?
Kid: Ice cream!
Dad: Me too. Wish we had some dessert.

Q: Why couldn't the tennis shoe talk to the high heel?
A: They didn't share a common tongue.

Beethoven had one major rule
about composing:
If it ain't Baroque, don't fix it.

___

Did you hear about the Marine who got arrested after a wild night on the town?
He was embarrassed to the Corps.

___

Q: Why are pine trees so irritating?
A: They're always needling you.

___

Did you hear about the dad who went to a housewarming party?
He adjusted the thermostat and left.

Jacob loved to eat beans, but one day he made the mistake of eating them before dinner with his girlfriend Sami's family. On the drive over, he started to feel uncomfortably gassy. At Sami's parents' house, Jacob gingerly sat down across from Sami's grandmother at the dining table. Feeling a huge fart building in his gut, he held it in as long as possible. Meanwhile, he lured the family's dog, Scruff, with scraps of food under the table. When Jacob couldn't hold back any longer, he aimed the horrendous fart toward Scruff, hoping that everyone would blame the pooch.

Sure enough, Sami's father wrinkled his nose, turned to the dog, and said with disgust, "Scruff!"

"Oh, good!" Jacob thought. "They think it's the dog!" As they dined, he felt another powerful stinker coming on. Finally, he let it rip. The horrific smell permeated the dining room.

This time, Sami's mother looked under the table and shouted, "Scruff!"

Soon, Jacob felt more gas pains. He let out another awful, hair-curling fart. Suddenly, the grandmother got down, pulled the dog away from the table, and hovered over him protectively. "Scruff, get out from under Jacob before he poops on you!"

Q: Which rock group has four men who can't sing?
A: Mount Rushmore.

Knock-knock!
Who's there?
Uriah.
Uriah who?
Keep Uriah the ball, slugger!

It's hard to hang around with harpists.
They're very high strung.

Q: Where do mermaids sleep?
A: On waterbeds.

 I'm a huge gaming nerd, and people have been telling me to get a life. But that's dumb. I have *lots* of lives.

A hobbit tried to write his memoir.
But it wound up a short story.

Man #1: How's sober life?
Man #2: I thought I was a mean drunk, but it turns out I'm a mean person.

Free-range parenting is the best. I like to range freely until I'm far away from my kids.

Q: What's pink, slippery, and sings "Mrs. Robinson"?
A: Salmon and Garfunkel.

My sixth-grader was complaining that at school the other day, she had to play soccer with third-graders. I told her if the school was really that hard up for money, I'd donate during the next fundraiser.

"What do you mean?" she asked.

I said, "Well, don't you think they should invest in a few soccer balls?"

Q: Why is Peter Pan always flying?
A: He neverlands.

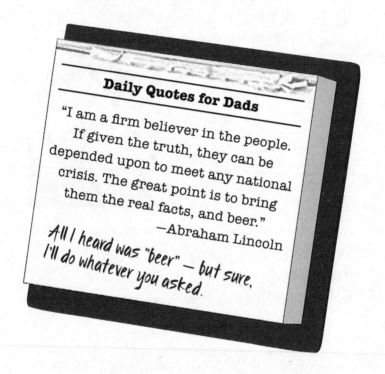

Daily Quotes for Dads

"I am a firm believer in the people. If given the truth, they can be depended upon to meet any national crisis. The great point is to bring them the real facts, and beer."

—Abraham Lincoln

All I heard was "beer" — but sure, I'll do whatever you asked.

After decades of hanging around with Peter Pan, Tinker Bell moved on.
She started a ferry service.

Did you hear that a bunch of cookies formed a soft rock band?
It's called OREO Speedwagon.

The hikers weren't sure if the tree was a dogwood or not. It was hard to tell from the bark.

Q: Why did the basketball player sit on the sideline and sketch pictures of turkeys?
A: He was trying to draw fowls.

You can never win a game against a porcupine. It'll always have the most points.

I recently went on an easy ski trip. I got off the chairlift, and it was all downhill from there.

Husband: I saw Al Gore do the robot dance!
Wife: Really? How'd he do?
Husband: He followed the Al Gore rhythm.

Q: Who is Jon Bon Jovi's fishy cousin?
A: Ann Jovi.

Knock-knock!
Who's there?
Watson.
Watson who?
Watson TV tonight?

Q: Who was Alexander Graham Bell's
grandma?
A: Alexander Grandma Bell.

 Kid: Dad, can you tell me the
technical name for a throwing star?
Dad: Shuriken!

I'm going to Seattle.
I've been wondering how Attle is doing.

Child: Dad, where are we going?
Dad: Craaaaazy!

Q: What do pirates snack on when they're at sea?
A: Swordines.

I know that if my mom fell and screamed for help, my dad would jump right up to rescue her as soon as it was halftime.

—Bruce Cameron

Q: Does Snow White like her friends?
A: Yeah, but one is a little Dopey.

Q: Where does everyone sit at the beginning of a tennis match?
A: In love seats.

You know that bird feeder in your backyard? It's just a place for seedy characters to gather.

@KentWGraham

I finally got some me time away from the kids. Two whole hours. It would've been longer but my legs went numb crouching behind the dryer.

A major league baseball player sits down for an interview with a reporter. They discuss his favorite athletes, what inspired him to become a ballplayer, and what advice he'd give to young players. Finally, the reporter asks, "What three things would you want people to say about you after you're gone?"

He thinks for a moment before answering. "At my memorial, I hope that my family recalls that I was a wonderful husband and father. I'd want my fans to say that I'm not only talented, but inspiring—that I made a difference in their lives. But most of all," he continues, as the reporter leans in, "I'd want someone at my funeral to say about me, 'Look! He's moving!'"

Did you hear about the cartooning contest?
There was no winner. It was a draw.

———

*My daughter just turned 4,
so she loves visiting aquariums and
going to the beach—anything related
to water. I'll sometimes try to get her to
wash my car, but she's not into that
kind of water activity.*

—Randall Park

———

For my friend's birthday, I got him
a telepathic abacus.
It's the thought that counts.

———

Batman walks into a bar.
"What'll you have?" the
bartender asks.
　Batman growls,
"Just ice."

```
:)
-------------
Sweetie,
what's that?
-------------
A smiley face.
Welcome to
the future,
Grandpa!
-------------
But it looks
like an ear
```

Q: What do cavemen eat for lunch?
A: Club sandwiches.

Everybody has a hidden talent, even me.
I just wish I could find mine.

Son: What do you need to get at the hardware store?
Dad: The hardware store will tell me.

> **@NewDadNotes**
>
> My daughter just walked over and pulled a potato chip from my hoodie pocket and ate it. I have so many questions.
>
>

My mother was extremely overprotective.
As kids, we were allowed to play
"Rock, Paper, Paper."

Something I'll never understand: how come smoking kills people, but it cures salmon?

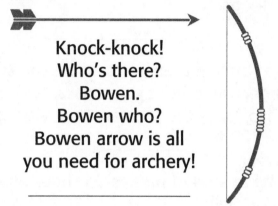

Knock-knock!
Who's there?
Bowen.
Bowen who?
Bowen arrow is all
you need for archery!

Q: Why is roller blading a good hobby?
A: It keeps you in line.

Q: When's the best time to go skydiving?
A: Fall.

I went to a restaurant, and it had Salisbury steak on the menu. I excitedly called over the waiter and asked him to wipe it off.

Q: What kind of earrings do basketball players wear?
A: Hoops.

As a Russian prepares to cross the Ukrainian border, the border guard asks, "Occupation?" "No," says the Russian. "Just visiting."

Q: What kind of parties do shoes attend?
A: Footballs.

Q: How does a drum set feel after a concert?
A: Beat!

"Boys will be boys, and so will a lot of middle-aged men."
—Kin Hubbard

Me and this recliner?
Oh yeah, we go way back.

Wife: What are you gonna do today?
Husband: Nothing.
Wife: You did that yesterday.
Husband: I didn't finish.

 @byclintedwards

Daytime parenting: strict screen time limits. 1hr only. Child must earn it.

5am parenting (hands 4yo iPad): take this so I can sleep.

Did you hear about the brother and sister ants who sang sad soft rock songs?
    They were Carpenter ants.

"You're not a real magician at all," Tom said, disillusioned.

Q: Why did the boy magnet like the girl magnet?
A: She was undeniably attractive.

Kid: How did you learn to play golf?
Grandpa: I took a golf course.

Did you hear about the sad cruise ship?
It was a woe boat.

Knock-knock!
Who's there?
Quentin.
Quentin who?
Quentin my thirst by drinking
out of your garden hose.

———————

Several Romans walk into a bar.
"Five beers," one says, holding up two fingers.

———————

A rabbi organized a charity fundraiser and was disappointed by the lack of interest from his congregants. Instead of helping the less fortunate members of their community, they were blowing their money on booze, gambling, and frivolities. Every day, the rabbi prayed that the rich congregants in his synagogue would share their money with the poor people who needed it.

A week later, his wife asked him, "How is the fundraiser going? Has your prayer been answered?"

"Half of it was," replied the rabbi. "The poor are willing to accept the money."

I started reading a book about antigravity.
I wasn't sure I'd like it, but I just can't
put it down!

Q: How do astronauts pass the time?
A: They play Moonopoly.

If a bird becomes an insult
comic, then that makes it...
a mockingbird!

I spotted a beer in danger the other day.
It wasn't breathing, so I gave it
mouth-to-mouth.

Q: Why don't crabs go out at night?
A: They're hermits.

Kid: Want to play football?
Dad: Sure, but let me take off my glasses.
Kid: How come?
Dad: It's a contact sport.

Q: What do you get when you cross a big happy dog with a metal detector?
A: A gold retriever.

Q: Why do you have to be careful at poker rooms in the jungle?
A: There are so many cheetahs.

A lack of general knowledge is my Achilles' knee.

A soccer hooligan stood before a judge, charged with disorderly conduct and assault. A police officer testified that he saw the accused throw something off a cliff just down the road from the stadium.

"What did you see the man throw?" asked the judge.

"Stones, your honor."

Confused, the judge said, "That isn't a crime, is it?"

"Normally not," the officer admitted. "But Stones is the name of the soccer referee."

 @jurisdoc741

93% of parenthood is saying "that's great" to whatever thing your kid is showing you on YouTube.

Q: What country has the most chess grand masters?

A: The Check Republic.

"I've located the Dog Star," Tom said seriously.

I poured root beer in a square glass.
Now I just have beer.

Neighbor: Do you like fly fishing?
Dad: It's oh-fish-ally the best sport ever!
Neighbor: What's so great about it?
Dad: I don't know, you just get hooked.

Q: Which country produces the fastest runners?
A: Russia.

Did you hear that a beluga attended the royal wedding?
He was the Prince of Whales.

The perfect bean soup recipe calls for 239 beans. If it had one more, it would be too farty.

Q: Why can't you play with Legos in outer space?
A: They might get sucked into a block hole.

_____

Wife: Care for a meat ball?
Husband: No thanks, I'd rather play with a rubber one.

_____

Q: What do unicorns eat for breakfast?
A: Horn Flakes.

_____

A limbo champion walks into a bar.
   He's no longer the limbo champion.

BAD ADVICE FROM A REAL DAD

"If you're going to do something stupid, don't get caught. You'll only be in trouble if you get caught."

Q: What do you call a dry piece of cake?
A: The Sahara Dessert.

If you are what you eat, then my dog is newspaper, used tissues, week-old crumbs on the kitchen floor, whatever he finds in the cat's litter box, some leaves, and a sock.

Great Moments in Dad History

June 11, 1988: Martin "Marty" Dunder is the first dad to strap on a fanny pack. (He also wears black socks with sandals, completing the ultimate dad look.)

Q: How do football players eat their cereal?
A: From a super bowl.

I sent ten of these jokes to ten of my friends, hoping that at least one would make somebody laugh.
   No pun in ten did.

One Sunday night, three football fans drowned their sorrows at their local bar after yet another loss by their favorite team. The first fan said, "This is all the coach's fault. If he had better plays, we'd have a great team!" The second fan said, "Well, I blame the players. They're lazy and don't try hard enough." The third fan thought for a second and said, "I blame my parents. If I'd been born in New England, I'd have a much better team!"

 @LetMeStart

I'm back from a weekend away with the kids.
Notice I did not use the word "vacation"?
That was deliberate.

I'm not like other dads.
Sure, I mow the lawn every Saturday,
but I don't really enjoy it.

Q: Why did the racehorse owners name their best horse Frozen Orange?
A: Because he's a sherbet.

Knock-knock!
Who's there?
Rhoda.
Rhoda who?
Rhoda bike with my kid all day, and I'm so tired!

Q: What do you call a black horse wearing venetian blinds?
A: A zebra.

You know you're a dad when you shake your handful of candies before you drop them in your mouth.

Q: What do you call a Pokémon character who can't move very fast?
A: A slowpoke.

Waitress: Soup or salad?
Dad: Super salad? I'll just have a regular one.

Q: What has two beards and rocks?
A: ZZ Top.

 @rcromwell4

It was bittersweet tearing down my kids'
swing set and trampoline knowing the
hours of enjoyment they got from other
things while those sat unused.

I bought a coffee table book about
the history of forests.
I just like to leaf through the pages.

Q: Why was the horse from Kentucky so
generous with his horse friends?
A: Southern horspitality.

Q: What did the cowboy's horse say when it fell down?

A: "I've fallen, and I can't giddyup!"

Yoga instructor: Yoga is a wonderful way to relax!

Me: Only if you close your eyes and imagine yourself lying in bed watching TV and not doing yoga.

I watched ice hockey before it was cool. It was called "swimming."

Laziness is nothing more than the habit of resting before you get tired.

—Jules Renard

Q: Why do scuba divers fall backward out of the boat?

A: Because if they fell forward, they'd still be in the boat.

Girlfriend: This restaurant's waiters are as terrible as its website.
Boyfriend: I guess it just has a problem with servers.

Q: What does Thor wear under his costume?
A: Thunderpants.

Waiter: Do you want a box for your burger?
Dad: No, but I'll wrestle you for the fries!

Q: Why did the beach smell like urine?
A: Because the sea weed.

Knock-knock!
Who's there?
Rita.
Rita who?
Rita book—you might learn something.

"Another plate of steamers all around!"
Tom clamored.

Q: What do baseball players wear on their knees?
A: Kneecaps.

This bouncy castle used to cost
half as much to rent.
I blame inflation.

---

*Remember: what dad really wants
is a nap. Really.*

—Dave Barry

Little Jessa's parents were regular churchgoers.
One afternoon, the reverend stopped by their
home. While Jessa's mother made snacks
in the kitchen, she sent Jessa to keep the
reverend company in the living room. For a
few minutes, Jessa stared at him intently. "Is
anything wrong, child?" the reverend asked.

"No," said Jessa, never taking her eyes
off him.

"Is there a reason you're watching me?"

"I want to see you gulp the ocean!"

"Do what?" replied the reverend, confused.

"My dad says you drink like a fish!"

Q: What's a good snack for dads?
A: Pop-corn.

Somebody threw a football at
President Trump.
A Secret Service agent shouted,
"Donald, duck!"

Kid: What do you do when you get thirsty at a baseball game?
Uncle: Ask for a pitcher.

Q: Why did the chili competition get shut down?
A: There was a gas leak.

Q: What do ninjas and farts have in common?
A: The quieter they are, the deadlier they are.

You know you're a dad when you feel the desire, nay, the *need* to buy a riding lawn mower.

Q: What do thirsty alligators drink?
A: Gatorade.

Q: How do tubas brush their teeth?
A: With a tuba toothpaste.

I wanted to wish my dad a happy Father's Day today. But he has a flight on Labor Day and already left for the airport to beat traffic.

DAD'S RECIPE FOR A
LEMON DROP COCKTAIL

1. DROP A LEMON.

Q: What kind of pants make music?
A: Bell bottoms.

Q: Why do boulders listen to heavy metal?
A: Because it rocks!

 @danjan13

I gazed upon the ocean for the first time and felt calm, like a dad staring at the yard for some reason.

Cinderella certainly impressed the prince upon her arrival at the ball. After all, she had a really great coach.

Q: What did Beethoven call his own farts?
A: Classical gas.

I didn't care for that movie about the maple tree. It was too sappy.

Q: What's a good name for a hamburger?
A: Patty.

Q: What should you wear to a tea party?
A: A tea shirt.

Great Moments in Dad History

April 19, 1977: Upon being greeted with "Hi, I'm Beth, and I'll be your waitress" at a restaurant, Jerry Coy is the first man to respond, "Hi, I'm Dad, and I'll be your customer!"

Wife: This brownie is a lot like you.
Husband: Aww, because it's sweet?
Wife: No, because it's a little stale and very nutty.

Q: What flowers do ragtime musicians use to freshen their breath?
A: Jazz mints.

Q: What do you call a cold burrito?
A: A brrrr-ito.

Beer makes you feel the way you ought to feel without it.

—Henry Lawson

Q: What's the laziest food?
A: Bread. All it does is loaf.

Knock-knock!
Who's there?
Fred.
Fred who?
Fred chicken for dinner tonight!

My dog can catch a ball from five miles away.
I know it sounds far-fetched.

Her: This hotel room is too cold.
Him: Go in the corner. It's 90 degrees!

I was playing a regular game of baseball with my dad. Until he threw me a curveball.

Brunch is the best meal. It's eggs-cellent.

Apple representative: Have you tested out the new iPhone?
Microsoft rep: No, actually, I haven't.
Apple rep: Neither have we!

I told my teenaged son that I think *Fortnite*
is a stupid name for a computer game.
It's just too week.

 @thedad

Laughing at a child's joke is a great way
to hear that exact same joke 8,000 more
times.

I used to be in a band with a lemon.
We kicked him out because he hit too many
sour notes.

Steve Harvey got in an argument
with his father.
It was a Family Feud.

Q: How does Reese eat soup?
A: Witherspoon.

I'm not like other dads.
Sure, I drive a minivan, but I listen to the
college rock radio station.

Kid: Hey, my fortune cookie is empty!
Dad: That's unfortunate.

Q: What did Sherlock Holmes say when his crime-fighting partner grew a mustache?
A: "Watson your face?"

Knock-knock!
Who's there?
Al.
Al who?
Al tell you my Netflix password
if you let me play your video games.

Q: What did the scuba diver say when he needed more air?
A: "Tanks!"

Q: Why do scuba divers sleep so quietly?
A: They use a snore kill.

Q: Where do people learn to make the best ice cream?
A: In sundae school.

 @DadandBuried

Am I proud of myself for letting my kids wake up, play video games, and watch YouTube for 5 hours every summer morning? No.
But am I going to get out of bed and organize activities so they can have fun experiences and we can spend quality time together as a family? Also no.

I fell into a hole at the beach
filled with razor shells.
It made my skin all clammy.

I don't like French food.
It gives me the crepes.

Q: Where does the Six Million Dollar Man live?
A: In a six-million-dollar mansion.

Josh was walking home from his neighbor's
Halloween party when he heard a strange
noise behind him. *Thump, thump, thump,
thump.* When he turned around, he saw an
upright coffin thumping down the street.
Nervously, Josh started walking faster,
but he still heard *thump, thump, thump,
thump* behind him. Soon he was running,
and the coffin picked up the pace, too.
Thumpthumpthumpthump. Then Josh ran for
his life, faster than he ever had before. The
coffin was right on his heels! "Help!" Josh
screamed, but no one responded. At last,
he made it to his house. He dashed inside
and tried to slam the door, but the coffin
got in, too. Up the steps Josh ran, with the
coffin following. *Thumpthumpthumpthump!*
Josh dashed into the bathroom and started
grabbing things to throw at the coffin as it

neared the top of the staircase. A hair dryer, razor, toothpaste—he lobbed them all at the coffin to no avail. Now the coffin loomed in the doorway, blocking his escape. Desperate, Josh tossed some cough drops at the coffin... and finally the coffin' stopped.

People say I'm living in a fantasy world. But they're just jealous of my talking unicorn.

Q: How do you make a root beer float?
A: Throw a root beer in the ocean.

Q: What do you call six guys staring at a steak?
A: A neighborhood cookout.

I love sports analogies.
They're a home run!

"Company should be here in about an hour," Tom guessed.

Q: Why did the man visit the sauna?
A: He needed a boost of self a-steam.

Q: Why wasn't the colt a very good singer?
A: He was a little horse.

Want to hear a joke about drills?
Never mind, it's a dull bit.

Q: What do you call a French guy who wears cheap sandals?
A: Phillippe Phillope.

Tourist #1: Why do they call it the Eiffel Tower?
Tourist #2: Because it's an eyeful.

Spring's here! I'm so excited
that I just wet my plants.

Q: What does Shrek wear under his arms?
A: De-ogre-ant.

"Coffee must make you sleepy.
They're always sleepy when they drink it."

Kid: Dad, do you have a sweet tooth?
Dad: Nope. I've got a whole mouth full!

Q: Where does Marilyn Manson live?
A: In his Maryland mansion.

A pastor campaigned against alcohol, which he called the scourge of mankind. One Sunday, he went to a bar looking for people to convert to his cause. Recognizing a man from his neighborhood, the pastor asked, "Hey, Jim, do you want to go to heaven?"

The man replied, "Yes, Pastor, of course."

The pastor said, "Then put down that scotch, go out front, and wait for me to lead us to the church. I have a special sermon today." Jim did as he was told.

Then the pastor asked Jim's friend, "You want to go to heaven, too, don't you?"

"I do, Pastor," the man replied.

"Then put down that beer, go outside, and wait for me," said the pastor. The man did so.

Seeing one of his congregants, the pastor approached the man and asked, "Bruce, do you want to go to heaven?"

Alarmed, Bruce said, "No, I don't, Pastor."

The pastor recoiled. Speaking slowly, he said, "Do you really mean that when you die, you want to go to hell?"

"Oh, when I die! Yes, I want to go to heaven," Bruce replied. "I thought you were getting a group together to go right now."

Why I like bowling so much:
1. I drink beer.
2. I get a few seconds of exercise.
3. I repeat #1 and #2 for the next couple of hours.

> **@Death_Buddy**
>
> *walks outside*
>
> Its real quiet.. Almost too quiet.
>
> *looks around*
>
> *lights BBQ*
>
> *1000 Dads emerge from nowhere giving generic BBQ advice*
>
>

My daughter requested a bedtime story about horses. So I gave her a ponytail.

When I was a kid, I figured that one day I'd have to stop playing video games and riding a skateboard.

And then I heard about being a dad.

FOR YOUR HEALTH
Fitness, Aging, and Eventual Death

I'm going to start dieting next week.
Right now I'm in the weighting period.

> **@KevinFarzad**
>
> I think it's sweet that teens text "U up?"
> really late at night to check that their
> friends are getting to bed at a reasonable
> hour
>
>

Patient: Doctor, will I live a long time?
Doctor: I think you'll live to be 60.
Patient: But I *am* 60!
Doctor: See?

They say that exercise is like a drug.
And I don't do drugs.

A horse with a bandage on his head limps into a bar. He orders four beers, downs them all, and says to the bartender, "I really shouldn't be drinking with what I've got."

"What have you got?" the bartender asks. The horse answers, "About fifty cents."

"We are communicating better, but we are still not out of the woods."

I got really sick when I was in Rome and had to check into a hospital. They put me on a 4 drip.

Q: Which infamous military general wasn't left-handed or right-handed?
A: Benedict Arnold. He was underhanded.

———

I shouldn't have eaten the seafood
that had been sitting out.
Now I'm feeling eel.

———

Q: What do sprinters eat before a race?
A: Nothing. They fast.

———

You know you're a dad when you grunt
getting up *and* sitting back down.

———

LIES DADS TELL

"I feel just as good now as I did when I was 20!"

"Yes, Doctor, I've avoided sweets."

"Nonalcoholic beer tastes just as good as the real thing."

My dad had the greatest facial hair.
Not just great, it was fan-stache-tic.

Dad: What's wrong?
Kid: I stubbed my toe, and it really hurts!
Dad: I'll tell you what...
Kid: Okay...
Dad: Better not do that anymore.

Q: Why did the guy sit on the copier and take a picture of his rear end?
A: He was getting behind in his work.

Wife: How do you feel?
Husband: Same as always. With my hands.

 @Cheeseboy22
I bet when I'm driving a minivan, folks say, "There's a dad" but when I've got my window down & elbow out, they say, "THERE'S A COOL DAD!"

Parenting an only child is a lot like
how the solar system works.
Everybody orbits the son.

_____

Girl: Why did my brother's tooth fall out?
Grandma: Because it was looth.

_____

I thought about going on an all-almond diet.
But that's just nuts.

Knock-knock!
Who's there?
Vicky.
Vicky who?
Vicky to good health is a balanced diet.

Q: What did the green grape say to the purple grape?
A: "Breathe!"

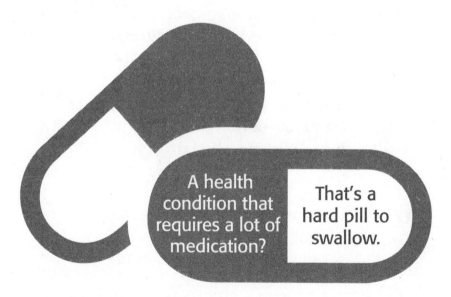

A health condition that requires a lot of medication? That's a hard pill to swallow.

"The doctors removed a bone from my arm," said Tom humorlessly.

Kid: Dad, did you get a haircut?
Dad: No. I got them all cut.

An elderly man put a bunch of items on the conveyor belt at the checkout: cotton balls, cotton swabs, medicated powder, cold cream, and denture cleaner. First he tried to pay with a gift card for an auto shop. Then he wrote a check, and on the memo line he wrote, "Repairs."

An English teacher had a serious gastrointestinal problem that required surgery. After it was all over, she had a semicolon.

The phoenix is a mythical bird
that rises from the dead.
But only after making a complete
ash of itself.

Q: What rhymes with *boo* and stinks?
A: You!

Did you hear about the old guy who found his suppository in his ear?

No telling where he put his hearing aid.

A pirate goes to a doctor and says, "I've got all these moles on me back, arrr."

The doctor says, "Don't worry, they're benign."

The pirate replies, "Arrr, thar be ten, not nine!"

Daily Quotes for Dads

"Aging is not lost youth but a new stage of opportunity and strength."
—Betty Friedan

LIKE THE OPPORTUNITY TO SAY, "CAN YOU OPEN THIS JAR? I DON'T HAVE THE STRENGTH."

I'm on a 30-day diet.
So far, I've lost 15 days.

Dad: You know, I can chop a log just by looking at it.
Kid: No way!
Dad: I'm serious. I saw it with my own eyes.

Knock-knock!
Who's there?
Raoul.
Raoul who?
Sometimes you just have to
Raoul with the punches.

 @KeetPotato

doc: "your dad's been in a coma for 9
days, we're running out of ideas"

me: "let me try" [goes to adjust
thermostat]

dad: [opens one eye]

A father brought his young son to visit the widow of a family friend who had recently died. As they reached the front door, the dad said, "Now, Son, remember to tell Mrs. Jenkins how sorry you are."

"Why?" the kid replied. "I didn't kill him."

A town had a church bell that was rung every hour. One day, the bell rope broke, and the minister couldn't find anyone to fix it. Finally, a man came by to offer his services. He had a freakishly large head and a skull as hard as steel. "I heard the bell rope is broken," he said, his giant head bobbing. "I can be your new bell ringer."

The minister was doubtful. "This is very important," he explained. "The bell must be rung every hour between 6 a.m. and 9 p.m. How can you do that with the broken rope?"

"I have it all figured out," the visitor said as he nodded his huge head enthusiastically.

"It's almost noon," the minister pointed out. "Could you show me?"

Instead of walking up the stairs of the bell tower, the man sprinted up the spiral staircase, faster and faster until he achieved enough momentum to ram his giant head into the bell. The ringing echoed through the town. "You're hired!" said the minister.

Every day, from morning 'til night, the man rang the bell. The locals came to respect and adore him. One day, during a rainstorm, the man was dashing up the staircase to ring the bell. He slipped on the wet stairs, tumbled over the side of the staircase, and fell to his death.

Two townspeople rushed over. One asked, "Who is that?"

The second responded, "I never learned his name, but his face sure rings a bell."

The bell ringer's funeral was attended by everyone in town. Afterward, a familiar-looking man approached the minister. "The bell ringer was my brother," the newcomer said. The resemblance was obvious: This man also had a giant head with a skull as hard as steel. "After seeing how beloved he was and how kind everyone is here, I'd like to be your new bell ringer," the brother said. Delighted, the minister agreed.

The new bell ringer was just as dependable as his brother. But soon there was another downpour. As the bell ringer raced up the stairs, he slipped, tumbled over the railing, and fell to his death.

The same two townspeople rushed over. The first asked, "Do you know him?"

The second replied, "Not really, but he's a dead ringer for his brother."

Q: What kind of milk do pampered cows give?
A: Spoiled milk.

We don't devote enough scientific research to finding a cure for jerks.
—Bill Watterson

Two men sit in a bar drinking. One of them notices two old guys on the other side of the room and says, "Hey look, that's us in 20 years."

His friend looks up, laughs, and says, "No, that's us now. That's a mirror."

I called the incontinence hotline.
They asked me to hold.

Q: How come suntanning never caught on as a competitive sport?
A: Because the best you can ever get is bronze.

Did you hear about the guy who ate four cans of alphabet soup?
He had a very large vowel movement.

I saw an envelope on fire.
Don't worry, I stamped it out.

Great Moments in Dad History

October 1, 1969. Tom Wilkie is the first dad to hear a distant siren and say to his kid, "Hey, they're coming for ya!"

Did you hear about the hamster that died from not getting any exercise?
He lacked the wheel to live.

"I'm not fat!" Tom denied stoutly.

Q: What disease does an old roof get?
A: Shingles.

A man goes to a doctor and tells him, "Doc, I'm happy with my life and want to be around as long as possible. How can I live to be 100 years old?"

The doctor thinks for a minute. Looking the patient right in the eye, he says, "If you do all of these things without fail, you should be able to achieve your goal."

"Great!" the man says. "Just tell me what to do!"

"First, stop eating anything that tastes good. No more burgers, pizza, or ice cream. For you, it's all kale and smoothies now. You're also going to have to exercise at least four hours a day to counteract your metabolism. If you feel you don't have time, you must spend less time with your family, watch less TV—whatever it takes." The patient looks dismayed but is taking notes. The doctor continues, "Good news: you can still drink. But no more beer or cocktails. Once a week, you can have half a glass of the most bitter red wine you can find."

"Wow," the man says. "If I do all that, I can happily live to be 100?"

"Wait," the doctor replies, "I didn't say anything about 'happily.'"

Q: What's the difference between a newborn baby and a really old man?
A: Depends.

I made this face, and it got stuck like that. My mom was right!

A man was rushed to the hospital. There, a specialist gave him the bad news that he had only six months to live.

Fortunately, the man didn't pay his hospital bill, so the doctor gave him another six months to live.

Let's all grab something to kill that fly with.
We'll be a SWAT team!

Sister: Does an apple a day really keep the doctor away?
Brother: If you've got good enough aim it does.

A guy told everyone on the internet that he had a beard, but then he posted a picture of himself, and he was totally clean-cut.
    What a bald-faced liar!

Q: What's another name for twins?
A: Womb-mates.

Remember: A bird in the hand…
will probably poop in your hand.

---

*If you are young and drink a great deal,
it will spoil your health, slow your mind,
make you fat—in other words,
turn you into an adult.*

—P. J. O'Rourke

Patient: I have a ringing in my ears.
Doctor: You shouldn't answer.

A man goes to his doctor. "I've had terrible constipation," he complains. "I haven't gone for weeks."

"Are you doing anything for it?" the doctor asks.

"I force myself to sit on the toilet for a half hour in the morning, and then another half hour in the evening."

"I meant do you take anything," the doctor clarifies.

"Oh," the man says. "Yeah, usually a magazine."

Q: Can you finish a marathon if you're sick?
A: Sure, if you've got a runny nose.

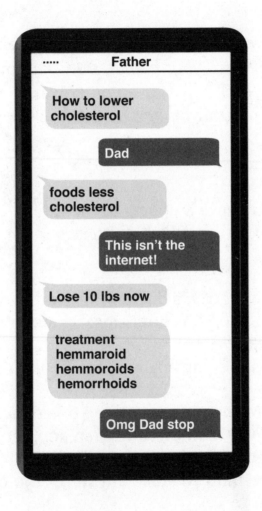

My kid just gave me my 50th birthday card. It's a nice gesture, but just one would have been fine.

Knock-knock!
Who's there?
Phyllis.
Phyllis who?
Phyllis cup with water, please.
I'm so thirsty!

We had a little accident the other day. I tried to explain to my three-year-old son that pooping your pants occasionally is perfectly normal. And yet he hasn't stopped making fun of me.

Wife: Going to lunch?
Husband: Yep.
Wife: Can I join you?
Husband: I didn't know I was falling apart!

My eyelids got really mad at me.
They lashed out!

A man walks into his psychiatrist's office. "Doctor, you've got to help me," he pleads. "Every night, I dream I'm a fast car. Last night, I dreamed I was a Trans Am. Another night, I was a Ferrari. Before that, I was a Porsche. What does it mean?"

"Relax," says the doctor. "You're just having an auto-body experience."

 @tonysheps
You know you're getting old when you watch Home Alone and wonder how much their mortgage is!

I used to always get little electric shocks whenever I'd touch a metal object.
But recently, it finally stopped.
It goes without saying, but I'm ex-static.

Did you hear Dracula went to the doctor?
He was coffin.

———————

A guy went to a dentist to have
some cavities worked on. His
regular dentist was on vacation,
so he had to settle for the
dentist who was filling in.

———————

My wife is really mad that I have no sense of
direction. She picked a big fight with me after
we got lost in a bad neighborhood. That was
the last straw. I packed up my stuff and right.

———————

Looking 50 is great. If you're 60.
—Joan Rivers

———————

My dad's convinced that the drugstore will be
the death of him, since sick people have to
walk all the way to the back of the store to
get their prescriptions while healthy people
can buy cigarettes right up front.

A man goes to the doctor for his yearly physical. The nurse asks some basic questions about his health. She begins with, "How much do you weigh?"

"Oh, about 150 pounds," the patient replies. He gets onto the scale, and his actual weight is 180.

Then the nurse asks, "What's your height?"

"Six feet tall," says the man. The nurse measures him, and he's only five foot nine.

"How's your blood pressure?"

"Good," he says. But when the nurse takes his blood pressure, it's extremely elevated. Before she can speak, he defends himself. "Of course it's high!" he shouts. "What did you expect? When I came in here, I was tall and thin, and now all of a sudden I'm short and chubby!"

I'm all about fitness.
Fitness extra meal in between
lunch and dinner.

Kid: Can I have your bookmark?
Dad: Sure, but you know my name is Ed.

"I'm losing my hair," Tom bawled.

Q: What's the worst part about working at a gas station?
A: All the burps and farts.

Always use the self-checkout line.
The cashiers are *so* good-looking!

A man steps onto a bathroom scale and sucks in his gut. His wife walks in and says, "You know, that's not going to help at all."

"Sure it is!" the man says. "I can see the numbers this way."

I've lost my mind. And I'm reasonably sure the kids took it.

Q: How do people who freeze up on the spot stay dry in the rain?
A: With an ummmmbrella.

Dogs can't see your bones. But cat scan!

I had a neck brace fitted years ago.
And I've never looked back.

A psychiatrist meets a new patient. "What's troubling you?" the doctor asks.

"I think I'm a goat," the patient responds.

"Okay," the doctor says, writing down some notes. "How long have you had this feeling?"

The man thinks about it before answering, "Ever since I was a kid."

Q: How come ointment never got a better job?

A: It wasn't good at applying itself.

Dock-dock!
Who's there?
A knock-knock joke with a cold.

Q: Why are tall people so optimistic?
A: They have high hopes.

Whenever someone calls me ugly,
I get really sad and give them a hug.
Life can be so tough when you're going blind.

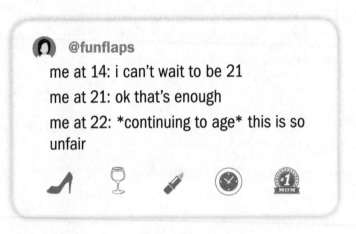

@funflaps

me at 14: i can't wait to be 21

me at 21: ok that's enough

me at 22: *continuing to age* this is so
unfair

Hostess: Sorry about your wait.
Dad: Me, too. I've really packed on the
pounds since college.

I always feel better when my doctor says something is normal for someone my age. Until I remember that at some point, death will be normal for someone my age.

My doctor says not to worry about
the bird flu. It's tweetable.

"I just got my gall bladder removed,"
said Tom, feeling rather disorganized.

Q: How do archers get in shape?
A: Arrowbics.

BAD ADVICE FROM A REAL DAD

"Coke is used to disinfect toilets,
so you can use it to clean wounds."

I think I have an inferiority complex.
But it's a terrible one.

Q: What do you call a pelican that isn't any
good at catching fish?
A: A pelican't.

Kid: Dad, have you seen my sunglasses?
Dad: No. Hey, have you seen my glasses?

I can't believe I forgot to go to the gym today. For 8,724 days in a row now.

THE SEVEN AGES OF MAN

1. spills
2. drills
3. thrills
4. bills
5. ills
6. pills
7. wills

I feel much like a square peg in a round hole. You could say I'm in bad shape.

After raising four kids, a woman reentered the workforce. Although she was not trained in medicine, she decided her experience as a mother qualified her to open a medical clinic. She guaranteed that she could treat any health problem for $250. A sign on her door read "If you're not cured, I'll give you $500."

One man thought this was a good opportunity to earn $500. Entering the clinic, he said, "Doctor, I've lost my sense of taste. Foods seem to have no flavor."

The woman called to her assistant, "Nurse, please bring medicine B24, and give the patient a half-ounce dose."

After the nurse fed him the medicine, the man exclaimed, "This is rubbing alcohol!"

The mom said, "Congratulations! Your sense of taste has been restored. That will be $250."

The customer got upset and concocted a plan to get his money back. A few days later, he walked in and said, "Doctor, I've lost my memory. I can't remember anything."

The mom called out, "Nurse, please bring medicine B24, and give the patient a half-ounce dose."

The man exclaimed, "But that's rubbing alcohol!"

The woman said, "Congratulations! You've got your memory back. That will be $250."

Angrily, the man stormed out. Later, he returned, saying, "Doctor, something is wrong with my eyes. I can barely see."

The woman thought for a moment and responded, "Well, I don't have a medicine for that. Take this $500."

Looking at the bills, the man protested, "But this is $250."

Snatching the money out of his hands, the woman said, "Congratulations! You got your vision back! That will be $250."

" Children are a great comfort in your old age, and they help you reach it faster, too. "

—Lionel Kauffman

Sadly, my dad passed away while we were traveling in a third-world country. At the hospital, we couldn't remember his blood type, so he didn't get the transfusion that would have saved his life. As he lay dying, he told us to "be positive," but we still miss him so much.

"I'm a self-taught doctor," Tom quacked.

Ryan Reynolds
@VancityReynolds

Being a father is the single greatest feeling on earth. Not including those wonderful years I spent without a child, of course.

Q: Why can't farts get a decent education?
A: Because they always get expelled.

Squatting down to get a beer off the
bottom shelf of the fridge
definitely counts as exercise.

Great Moments in Dad History

December 1, 1948. Tony Rainone is the
first dad to respond "red" when a nurse
asks him his blood type.

I felt so exhausted after giving blood.
It's really a draining procedure.

Q: What's tight, white, and full of holes?
A: Dad's underwear.

My doctor told me to eat more pizza.
Well, actually, she said to eat less red meat,
but that's pretty much the same thing.

One morning, a husband wakes up and rolls over to give his wife a kiss.

"Don't touch me!" she cries out. "I'm dead!"

"What do you mean?" he asks. "You can't be dead—you're lying here awake, and you're talking to me."

"I must be dead," she insists. "I woke up this morning, and it's the first time in years that nothing hurts."

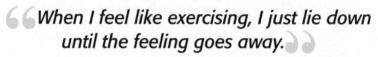

When I feel like exercising, I just lie down until the feeling goes away.

—Paul Terry

Did you hear about the failing student with bad gas?

He kept getting farter behind, so his parents hired him a tooter.

It's important to rest your muscles between workouts.
About three months is good.

Knock-knock!
Who's there?
Eyes darted.
Eyes darted who?
Eyes darted to droop, but I woke up!

Every machine at the gym does something different. What they all have in common is that you can take a nap on most of them.

Wife: You look ill.
Husband: I am. That was my fifth doughnut, and I regret it.
Wife: Of course you do. That's a *lot* of doughnuts.
Husband: No, I only regret the fifth one.

Sure, I exercised this month.
I ran out of money several times.

Did you hear about the man who didn't poop for months and then got diarrhea?
Talk about a blast from the past.

"Kids! Stop saying I have a dad bod!
I'd rather you call it a father figure."

The hardest I work out at the gym is when I'm looking for a parking spot.
You know, right up close by the door.

"Let's go for a walk now," said Tom stridently.

Daily Quotes for Dads

"As soon as you feel too old to do a thing, do it."
—Margaret Deland

Unless it's wearing leather pants. Because you'll probably look ridiculous.

Humming a happy tune, an elderly man rocked in a rocking chair on his porch. A woman approached him. "Excuse me," she said. "I couldn't help but notice how happy you look. What's your secret?"

"Every day, I smoke two packs of cigarettes, and I drink a bottle of whisky. I never exercise, and I eat all the fatty and sugary foods I want."

"Wow, that's...amazing," the woman said. "If you don't mind my asking, how old are you?"

"I'm 28."

Q: Why are dads hairier than moms?
A: They always have an extra 'stache at the
    ready.

Elderly man: I love this new hearing aid. It cost a ton of money, but it was worth it because it works great.
Friend: Oh yeah, what kind is it?
Elderly man: About 10:30.

Fifty is the age where you stop fooling yourself that if you just eat granola nobody will notice.

—Stephen King

Grandpa: Now that I'm a senior, when I lose my glasses they're usually not too far away.
Grandkid: Because you don't go many places anymore?
Grandpa: I meant because they're generally on my forehead.

Q: What did one strand of DNA say to the other?
A: "Nice genes!"

Knock-knock!
Who's there?
Blue.
Blue who?
Blue your nose on your sleeve again, huh?

Aging is half struggling to catch your breath
and half struggling to lose your breadth.

"My hair's been cut off," Tom said distressfully.

"I've determined the addictions that plague all of you," a psychologist announced to the support group he was leading. "Your obsessions can be seen in what you decided to name your children." Turning to one woman, he said, "You, ma'am, are addicted to money, which is why you named your daughter Penny." To another participant, the psychologist said, "You have a problem with food, which explains why your daughter is Candy." Another man got up and headed for the door with his son in tow. "This guy doesn't know what he's talking about," he said to his child. "Let's go home, Watching Golf on TV."

BAD ADVICE FROM A REAL DAD

"My dad told me one time that I shouldn't work out, because people who work out too much don't have the flexibility to lift their arms over their heads."

I'll never forget my first inoculation.
It was a real shot in the arm.

Q: Why did the chickens hit the gym?
A: To work on their pecks.

I was so nervous before my hernia surgery.
My stomach was in knots.

Q: What did the pirate say when his wooden
legs fell off during a blizzard?
A: "Shiver me timbers!"

---

*One of the good things about getting
older is you find you're more interesting
than most of the people you meet.*
—Lee Marvin

I like vegetables that are awesome,
but not *too* awesome.
Like the radish.

Grandma: Be kind to everyone.
Grandkid (scowling): Even my dentist?
Grandma: Yes, he has fillings, too.

You think I'm myopic? I just can't see it.

Wife: What a day!
Husband: How was your appointment?
Wife: I was diagnosed with Crohn's disease.
Husband: So, like, you're a witch?

 @CuriouslyEmily

An esteemed colleague told me he hard-boils eggs in the morning, uses them as pocket warmers, and then has them as a little mid-morning snack when he gets to work. Truly, the line between genius and madness is very thin.

I just read a book about proctology.
It had extensive end notes.

Patient: There's a problem with my knee.
Doctor: What is it?
Patient: My knee.
Doctor: I meant what happens to your knee?
Patient: It juts out in front of me.
Doctor: Oh, that's just a knee-jerk reaction.

Q: When you die, what's the last part of your body to shut down?
A: Your pupils. They dilate.

Middle age occurs when you are too young to take up golf and too old to rush up to the net.

—Franklin P. Adams

Knock-knock!
Who's there?
Dispense.
Dispense who?
Dispense are too tight—
I think I gained weight!

After I hurt my foot, I went to the podiatrist. But she just added insoles to injury.

Two pirates meet up in a pirate bar. The first one, Graybeard, has a patch over one eye, a hook for a hand, and a wooden peg leg.

"Ahoy!" says the other pirate, Long John. "What happened to ye since last I saw ye?"

"Arrr," says Graybeard. "Me pirate ship was attacked, and a lucky shot made me lose me leg. So now I got this peg."

"What about yer hand?" asks Long John.

"When me ship sank, a shark bit me hand off. Now I got me this hook."

"Why the eye patch?"

"I bes standin' on a dock, and the biggest seagull I ever saw poops in me eye."

"Ya went blind from seagull poop?"

"Nay," says Graybeard. "It was me first day with the hook."

My son didn't go to Harvard or Yale, but he's been to the hospital. That's why I tell people he went to an I.V. league institution.

Last night, my date said coyly, "I know the quickest way to a man's heart." Then she explained, "A sharp cut through the sternum with a bone saw."

I tripped and fell into a mirror the other day. I really ought to watch myself.

Husband: I'm not being lazy. It's called spontaneous relaxation.
Wife: It looks like laziness to me.
Husband: Well, then, I'm practicing self-care.

Dad: I bought a salad today.
Mom: Did you eat it?
Dad: Hey, baby steps.

Q: What makes a snake just lie there, not
moving around?
A: Reptile dysfunction.

I tried to tell my doctor the long story
about how I hurt my thumb.
It was all disjointed.

Brain surgeons are so ambitious.
They just want to get a head.

Q: What happened to the camper who came
down with Lyme disease?
A: He got really ticked off.

 @Dadpression

Pool noodles are a great way to sword
fight your kid while still lying on the
couch.

Patient: Doctor, how did you get so rich?
Doctor: I treat a lot of sick people.
Patient: Ah, so it's ill-gotten wealth!

We all want to belong.
But some of us are short.

———

Wife: Why are you just sitting in the dark? Are you feeling blue?
Husband: Yes, cyan.

———

Q: How do doctors make cosmetic surgery feel better?
A: An aesthetic.

———

"You know you've reached middle age when your weight lifting consists merely of standing up."

—Bob Hope

———

I'm afraid I can't work out today.
I just don't look very good in those stretchy yoga pants.

An upset patient called his doctor's office. When he reached the doctor, he blurted out, "Is it true that this medication you put me on has to be taken for the rest of my life?"

"Yes, I'm afraid so," the doctor answered.

Panicking, the man said, "Just tell me—how severe is my condition? Because this bottle is marked 'No refills'!"

 @EnglishJason

My daughter just asked why we say "hang up" the phone and now I feel 90.

Q: What do you call a snowman with a six-pack?

A: The abdominal snowman.

Traveler's tip from Dad:
Don't drink the water in foreign countries. Most of them have really good beer!

Chiropractors are great friends.
They always have your back.

_____

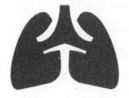 Lungs are just a pair of
windbags. If you're feeling
deflated, just take a breather.

_____

Knock-knock!
Who's there?
Ashley.
Ashley who?
Ashley's foot is making my feet all gross!

_____

"I've had my left and right ventricles
removed," Tom said half-heartedly.

_____

Did you hear about the optometrist who fell
into his lens-grinding machine?
He made a spectacle of himself.

_____

The terrible pain in my big toe finally
went away. No gout about it!

I rushed my wife to the hospital when she started to go into labor, but we didn't make it. She gave birth right there in the car.
It's a boy! We named him Carson.

Daily Quotes for Dads

"The longer I live, the more beautiful life becomes."
—Frank Lloyd Wright

OR AT LEAST I IMAGINE IT TO BE—I CAN'T SEE A THING WITHOUT MY GLASSES.

There's no definitive way to tell whether or not someone is colorblind. There's a lot of gray area.

Knock-knock!
Who's there?
Champ.
Champ who?
Champ poo your hair—it's filthy!

Wife: Looks like you're starting to go bald.
Husband: I beg to differ. I'm merely shedding my winter fur.

My girlfriend is feeling better after getting her appendix removed. Unfortunately, she will never be able to reference this chapter of her life.

"Try to get lots of sleep" is the part of a healthy lifestyle I can definitely get behind.

Q: What should you carry with you in case you get tired?
A: A knapsack.

The parents' version of "Head, Shoulders, Knees, and Toes" is "Snacks, Wallet, Keys, and Phone."

Patient: I'm thinking about getting a vasectomy, Doctor.
Doctor: Oh? That's a big decision. Have you discussed this with your family?
Patient: Absolutely. We took a vote, and we came down in favor of it, 15 to 2.

"That's the last time I'll pet a lion," Tom said offhandedly.

I was just minding my own business at the drugstore the other day when suddenly, out of nowhere, a stranger threw a bottle of omega-3 supplements at me. Fortunately, my injuries were only super fish oil.

Q: What kind of vehicles do podiatrists drive?
A: Toe trucks.

Patient: Doctor, I think my nose is finally clear!
Doctor: No, it's snot.

"Grapes are on sale. My grandma mentioned that in passing today, which was pretty random for someone's last words."

—Zach Reinert

Q: Why does lightning shock?
A: It doesn't know how to conduct itself.

Knock-knock!
Who's there?
Breed.
Breed who?
Breed deep and say "aah!"

Man: I went to the gym the other day, but they wouldn't let me in.
Friend: Why not?
Man: No ID!
Friend: Couldn't you at least ask?

@FatherWithTwins

Watched my 4yo make a potato chip sandwich with cookies for the bread, and now he's my new life coach.

I had the worst bladder infection the other day. At least I think so. The doctor just said, "Buddy, urine trouble."

———

Q: What do you call a man who has no nose and no body?
A: Nobody nose!

I decided not to have my son circumcised.
I had it done when I was a baby, and I
couldn't walk or talk for a year afterward!

BAD ADVICE FROM A REAL DAD

To a kid having an allergic reaction:
"There's no such thing as allergies.
If you keep eating nuts, your body will
eventually bend to your will."

"I've never had a car accident,"
said Tom recklessly.

I suffer from really bad allergies.
Just the worst you've ever encountered.
It's a pollen!

Q: Why should you never iron a four-leaf clover?

A: Because you don't want to press your luck.

_____

Q: Why was the Greek man not a morning person?

A: Because Dawn is tough on Greece.

 @WendiAarons

It's my son's last visit to the pediatrician, because he's almost 18, and also because on the form where they asked, "Do you own any weapons?" he wrote, "Only the guns I call my biceps."

Knock-knock!
Who's there?
Toothache.
Toothache who?
"Toothache the high road,
and I'll take the low road..."

Great Moments in Dad History

March 15, 1956: Augie DiCosimo is
the first dad to ever fall asleep on a couch
and then deny it, claiming to be
"just resting his eyes."

Do I use emoji? Yes, but I remember
the good old days, back when they
were called hieroglyphics.

Q: What do bald sea captains worry about?
A: Cap sizes.

A nail is the thing you aim at before you smack your fingers with a hammer.

Two dogs are going for a walk together, when one of them starts to unload all his problems. "My life is a mess," he says. "My owner is mean, my girlfriend ran away with a pit bull, and I'm more jittery than a cat."

"Why don't you go see a therapist?" suggests the other dog.

"I can't," the troubled dog says.

"Sure you can. I know a schnauzer who really calmed down after talking to someone."

"No, I mean I'm not allowed on the couch."

It's really easy to prevent women and kids from eating those Tide pods.
It's much tougher to deter gents.

A veterans' hospital nurse entered a patient's room to draw his blood. When she saw an apple on his desk, she quipped, "An apple a day keeps the doctor away! Isn't that right?"

"Yeah," he said. "In fact, come to think of it, I haven't seen a doctor all week."

 @gojarbe

[gun goes off]

[every runner pretends to be wounded, then laughs and starts the race]

ANNOUNCER: and the annual Dad 5k is underway

"Stop saying that I'm getting old!"
"Okay. You're nearing your expiration date."

YOU CAN'T MAKE THIS STUFF UP
Real-life Funnies

From a real court transcript:

Q: Now, your complaint alleges that you have had some problems with concentration since the accident. Does that condition continue today?

A: No, not really. I take a stool softener now.

Real note from a kid:

Dear Dad, can I do karate? I promise I won't hurt you. I could fight off robbers and it is great exercise.

Unfortunately Named Products from Around the World

- Barf Detergent (Iran)
- Batmilk Yogurt (Brazil)
- Pee Cola (Ghana)
- Plopp Caramel Chocolate (Sweden)
- Salticrax Crackers (South Africa)
- Bum Bum Ice Cream (Germany)

FUNNY HEADLINES

Study Reveals Those Without Insurance Die More Often

Suicide squirrels driving utilities nuts

Swiss Accidentally Invade Liechtenstein

GLOBAL WARMING RALLY CUT SHORT BY COLD WEATHER

North Korean Leader Names Ancient Frog "Ancient Frog"

British colonists in Malaysia created a game called hashing in the 1930s, and it's still played by locals. Hashing involves running, but it's not really a race. Participants start the event drunk, and then run through a five-mile maze. Every quarter mile there's a checkpoint with more booze, and confusingly, the course branches out into multiple routes. It doesn't even matter who wins—just who is able to finish and tell their story at the end of the race, which is usually at a bar.

What American Movies Were Called in Other Countries

U.S.: *Jaws*
France: *The Teeth from the Sea*

U.S.: *The Waterboy*
Thailand: *Dimwit Surges Forth*

U.S.: *Die Hard*
Spain: *The Glass Jungle*

U.S.: *Knocked Up*
Peru: *Slightly Pregnant*

U.S.: *The Dark Knight*
Venezuela: *The Knight of the Night*

———————————

"I have learned from my mistakes, and I am sure I can repeat them exactly."

—Peter Cook

———————————

On a sign outside a school:
Congradulation Spelling Bee Winners

Bumper sticker:
Wrinkled was not one of the things
I wanted to be when I grew up

 @HomeWithPeanut

I feel you Oscar the Grouch. If I had to
deal with that many kids all the time, I
would hide in a trash can as well.

SILLY WARNING LABELS SPOTTED ON PRODUCTS

On a can of insect spray:
"Harmful to bees."

On a box of sleeping pills:
"May cause drowsiness."

On a bag of peanuts:
"This product contains nuts."

On a mattress:
"Do not attempt to swallow."

On a chainsaw:
"Do not attempt to stop chain with hands
or genitals."

Presumably, half the customers were amused, and the other half's complaints fell on deaf ears, when a gas station put up this sign:

"My wife said I never listen to her, or something like that."

Euphemisms for Farting

Trouser trumpet	Booty cough
Duck call	Butt salute
Back draft	Frump
Air biscuit	Windy pop

Real Note Left on a Car Windshield

"I hit your car, I'm sorry! Because you looked rich, I'm not leaving my number."

Vanity License Plates

ITSYELLO (on a yellow car)
NOT COP (on a Crown Victoria)
OJ DID IT (on a white Ford Bronco)
NOT-POOR (on a Mercedes)
SORRY (on a car with Canadian plates)
SHELEFT (on a sports car)

McDonald's once created bubblegum-
flavored broccoli. (It was a flop.)

Sign at a high school:
School resumes Aug 20
Resistance is futile
You will be educated

My parent: "Someday, Son, this will all be yours."
Note to self: Find out how to write myself out of a will.

REAL U.S. COURT CASE NAMES

Frankenstein v. Independent Roofing & Siding
Big v. Little
Ruff v. Ruff
State v. Big Hair
Hamburger v. Fry

Punny Beer Names

Peter Cotton Ale
Yippie Rye Aye
Audrey Hopburn
Stop, Hop, and Roll
The Big Lebrewski
Smooth Hoperator
Peter Piper's Pickled Pepper Purple
Peated Pale Ale

Real Work Fridge Note

To the person who stole and drank my 20 oz. Dr. Pepper: I had already been drinking from that. Enjoy your new cold sore. I hope you enjoyed my drink because trust me, you will never forget it.

Epitaph Spotted at a Graveyard in Ireland

Wherever you be
Let your wind go free
For it was keeping it in
That was the death of me.

 @AndyHerald

According to toddlers, you haven't really said goodbye unless you've said it 20 or 30 times.

Real (And Really Odd) Book Titles

- *How Green Were the Nazis?*
- *The Stray Shopping Carts of Eastern North America: A Guide to Field Identification*
- *Better Never to Have Been: The Harm of Coming Into Existence*
- *People Who Don't Know They're Dead: How They Attach Themselves to Unsuspecting Bystanders and What to Do About It*

Sign at a San Diego library:
Summer readinng program

In the 1960s, the president of Rival dog food invited the press to lunch. He brought a guest—a pedigreed collie—who sat at the main table with him and was served Rival's new "all-beef dinner." It was smart advertising, except that the dog wouldn't eat the food, and wouldn't even sniff it. Panicking, the executive dug into the dog food and ate it himself to show how good it was. The next day, newspapers declared "RIVAL PRESIDENT EATS DOG FOOD, BUT DOG WON'T."

Strange But True
Official state beverage of Indiana: water

Guys are lucky because they get to grow mustaches. I wish I could. It's like having a little pet for your face.

—Anita Wise

From a real court transcript:
Q: And what was he wearing under the mask?
A: Uhh, his face?

Real note from a kid:
I won't love you if you make me clean my room

Keep Your Eye on the Goat Carcass
Popular in the central Asian countries of Afghanistan and Kyrgyzstan, buzkashi is a game similar to polo: Teams on horseback move an object past a goal line to score. But instead of a ball, buzkashi is played with a headless, limbless goat carcass weighed down with sand. To steal the carcass from the other team, players may trip horses or whip their opponents. And you thought hockey was rough!

Sign on the door of a bank in Wales:
Due to the weather we are closed.
Sorry for any incontinence

If you want your children to listen, try talking softly—to someone else.

—Ann Landers

Bumper sticker:
WHEN EVERYTHING IS COMING YOUR WAY,
YOU'RE IN THE WRONG LANE

English Subtitles from
Hong Kong Action Movies

"Fat head! Look at you! You're full of cholesterol."

"The tongue is so ugly. Let's imagine it to be Tom Cruise."

"It took my seven digestive pills to dissolve your hairy crab!"

"Dance the lion for others for just some stinking money! It's like razing my brows with the kung-fu I taught you."

"Alternatively, you must follow my advice whenever I say 'maltose.'"

@copymama

No one is as glued to any piece of reading material as a parent counting down the songs in the program of a really boring school concert.

On a billboard advertising a school:
ABC Chilren's Academy

Real Fridge Note

Dear Fridge Thief,
Please chop your
hands off, to save
me the trouble.
#leavemyfruitalone

Colorfully Named Pubs of Britain

Bull and Spectacles	The Thatcher's Foot
Donkey on Fire	The Drunken Duck
The Fool & Bladder	Ye Olde Bung Hole

Game Show Goof
Todd Newton: Bourbon whiskey is named after Bourbon County, located in what state?
Contestant: England.

—Press Your Luck

REAL QUIPS FROM FLIGHT CREW MEMBERS

"Any person caught smoking in the lavatories will be asked to leave the plane immediately."

"We'd also like to remind you to turn off your cellular phones, computers, video games, or any other electronic device that may interfere with the captain's pacemaker."

"Ladies and gentlemen, we have reached our cruising altitude of 30,000 feet, so I'm going to switch off the seat belt sign. Feel free to move about the cabin, but please try to stay inside the plane until we land."

"Sorry about the rough landing, folks. I'd just like to assure you that it wasn't the airline's fault; it wasn't the flight attendants' fault; nor was it the pilot's fault. It was the asphalt."

On a No Parking sign:
Violators Will Be Towed and Find $50

MORE REAL COURT CASE NAMES

- *Friends of Kangaroo Rat v. California Dept. of Corrections*

- *U.S. v. Pipe on Head*

- *United States of America v. 2,116 Boxes of Boned Beef, Weighing Approximately 154,121 Pounds, and 541 Boxes of Offal, Weighing Approximately 17,732 Pounds*

- *Schmuck v. Dumm*

 @GrantTanaka

son: hey dad

me: [picks up phone, dials 9] yes

son: now don't get mad

me: [dials 1] ok

son: do we have a fire extinguisher

me: [dials 1]

Unfortunate Tattoo Fails

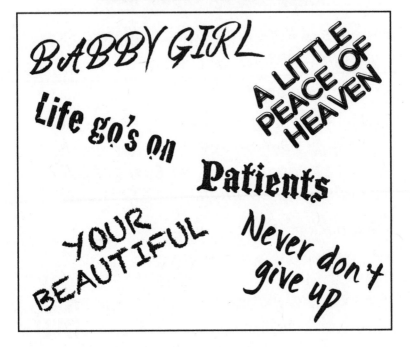

Bumper sticker:
99 Percent of Lawyers Give the Rest
a Bad Name

Game Show Goof
Alex Trebek: If a Japanese *isha* (doctor) asks
you to stick out your *shita*, he means this.
Contestant: What is…your behind?

—*Jeopardy!*

IF THEY MERGED

• If PolyGram Records, Warner Bros., and Cracker Barrel merged, they would become...*Poly-Warner-Cracker.*

• If 3M and Goodyear tires merged, the new company would be...*MMMGood.*

• If Denison Mines, Alliance Semiconductor, and Cedar Grove Mines merged, the new company would be...*Mine-All-Mine.*

• If Zippo Manufacturing, Audi, Mountain Dew, and Dakota Mining merged, the new company would be...*Zip-Audi-Dew-Da.*

Great Moments in Dad History

July 31, 1962. Larry McCloy becomes the first father to say, "Well, here's your mother" after talking to his grown daughter on the phone for 15 seconds.

LOONEY LAWS

- Playing with Silly String is against the law in Lodi, California.

- In Tennessee, it's illegal to sell bologna on Sundays.

- In Seattle, a dog must pay full bus fare if it weighs more than 25 pounds.

- It is against the law in Michigan for a lady to lift her skirt more than six inches while walking through a mud puddle.

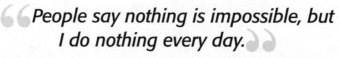

*People say nothing is impossible, but
I do nothing every day.*

—A.A. Milne's Winnie the Pooh

 @DadZZZasleep

Sick of my kids' ABC animal books having
to stretch for xenops and x-ray fish. Can we
just change "cat" to "xat" and move on?

Peculiar Palindromes

Lager, Sir, is regal.

A nut for a jar of tuna.

Lived on decaf, faced no devil.

He won a Toyota now, eh?

Draw putrid dirt upward.

Gary knits a stinky rag.

Did I strap red nude, red rump, also slap
murdered underparts? I did!

Cigar? Toss it in a can. It is so tragic.

Short-Lived Professional Wrestling Personas

- The Gobbledy Gooker. He was a giant turkey, complete with feathers, a beak, and wings. When the character debuted, he popped out of a huge egg.

- Giant Gonzales. A failed NBA basketball player, Gonzales was a lanky 7'7" and not muscular enough to wrestle. Solution: He wore a rubber suit covered with fake hair and painted muscles.

- Red Rooster. A guy with dyed scarlet hair who flapped his arms like wings and chicken-danced around the ring, screaming "cock-a-doodle-doo!"

- Isaac Yankem, DDS. An evil dentist, dressed in a white smock and face mask, who threatened to remove his opponents' teeth.

Actual Job Titles According to the US Department of Labor

Flocculator Operator
Ripening-Room Attendant
Round-up-Ring Hand
Bosom Presser
Bottom Buffer
Crown Pounder
Egg Smeller

Real note from a kid:
I think my dad is the most interesting person I know. It was easy to pick my dad over my mom because she's more like a regular mom.

From a real court transcript:
Lawyer: All right. I want to take us back to the scene at the bar for a moment again. [The witness gets up and starts to leave.] No, you don't have to get up. I just want to take you back there mentally.

Extremely Specific Online Dating Sites

ClownDating.com

H-date.com, for people with herpes

AmishDating.com

SingleswithFoodAllergies.com

RockabillyDate.com

MillionaireMatch.com, for rich people ("No Sugar Daddies/Babies")

VampireRave.com, for people who think they're vampires

Bumper sticker:
A journey of a thousand miles
begins with a cash advance

Ice Cream Flavors You Can Get in Japan

Fried chicken	Ox tongue
Miso	Lettuce-potato
Fish and brandy	Fried eggplant
Octopus	Squid ink

Dumb Jock Quotes

"Don't say I don't get along with my teammates. I just don't get along with some of the guys on my team."

—Terrell Owens, football player

"People think we make $3 million and $4 million a year. They don't realize that most of us only make $500,000."

—Pete Incaviglia, baseball player

"It's a humbling thing being humble."

—Maurice Clarett, football player

 @FU_TangClan
Is it really stealing if your kid doesn't know you got them the Easter Egg?

Real Fridge Note
(On a half-eaten slice of pizza)
"Just take the whole slice next time, okay?"

Shocking Collaboration

On his 2005 *Prince of Darkness* album, shock rocker Ozzy Osbourne does a version of the Steppenwolf song "Born to be Wild"…as a duet with Miss Piggy. Yes, the Muppet. Excerpt: "I like smoke and lightning," Osbourne sings. Miss Piggy squeals, "Oh, I do too!"

"I don't trust children. They're here to replace us."

—Stephen Colbert

LOONEY LAWS

- It's illegal to hunt moths under streetlights in Los Angeles.

- Geese may not walk down Main Street in McDonald, Ohio.

- In Chaseville, New York, it's against the law to drive a goat cart past a church in a "ridiculous fashion."

- A Tylertown, Mississippi, ordinance prohibits shaving in the middle of Main Street.

On a sign outside an elementary school:
LETERACY NIGHT

_____

More Euphemisms for Farting

Pop tart	Bull snort
Bean fumes	Blampf
Fizzler	Putt-putt
Benchwarmer	Cushion creeper

Real note from a kid:
Dad, I love you but you can't cut my hair, if you do I will never forgive you. I love my hair and guess you don't love me enough to do what I want for a change.

From a real court transcript:
Q: So, besides your wife and children, do you have any other animals or pets?

Famous People Anagrams

Paul McCartney	PAY MR CLEAN CUT
Bob Dylan	BLAND BOY
Robert De Niro	ERROR ON BIDET
Bill Murray	RUMBLY LIAR
Abraham Lincoln	HAIRBALL CONMAN
Nancy Reagan	AN ACE GRANNY
Sylvester Stallone	TALENTLESS SLY OVER
Albert Einstein	ELITE BRAIN NEST

In 2014 several residents reported seeing a huge snake near Lake Hopatcong in New Jersey. It was described by witnesses (who were clearly not snake experts) as a 10-foot long, or maybe 20-foot long, boa…or python…or anaconda. Photos of it were too grainy to tell for sure. Then someone started a Twitter account for the Hopatcong Anaconda, which gained hundreds of followers. Its posts revealed its daily life ("Crap! The dentist says I need braces. My life is ruined."), its pet peeves ("They're using an old photo of me. That was during my awkward teen phase. How embarrassing."), and its life in hiding ("Watching karate kid! Nobody knows I'm under this couch."). The snake was never caught.

Game Show Goof
Richard Dawson: Name something a blind man might use.
Contestant: A sword.

—Family Feud

Funny Vanity License Plates

VIAGRA (on a Corvette)
UNWED (on a Ferrari)
HON-DUH (on a Honda)
BKRPTCY (on a Bentley)
GEEZER (spotted in Florida)

"There is no sunrise so beautiful that it is worth waking me up to see it."
—Mindy Kaling

Colorfully Named Pubs of Britain

The Duke Without a Head
The Cat and Custard Pot
The Inn Next Door Burnt Down

MORE REAL QUIPS FROM FLIGHT CREWS

"As you exit the plane, please make sure to gather all of your belongings. Anything left behind will be distributed evenly among the flight attendants. Please do not leave children or spouses."

"Thank you for flying Business Express. We hope you enjoyed giving us the business as much as we enjoyed taking you for a ride."

"The next time you get the insane urge to go blasting through the skies in a pressurized metal tube, we hope you'll think of us."

Real Fridge Note

Before you judge a man, walk a mile in his shoes. After that, who cares? He's a mile away and you've got his shoes!

—Billy Connolly

 @KylieChamberss

is your dad really your dad if he doesn't say "who?" after talking about any of your friends even if he's known them for literally 7 years??

During the 1993 Super Bowl, the Buffalo Bills fumbled the ball on their own 45-yard line, where it was recovered by Dallas Cowboys lineman Leon Lett. He then did what few linemen ever do: He ran it all the way to the other end for a touchdown. As he was about to cross the goal line, he slowed down to celebrate, raising the ball in triumph…and it was knocked out of his hands by a Bills receiver hot on his tail. What a Lettdown.

LOONEY LAWS

- In West Virginia, only babies are allowed to ride in baby carriages.

- It's against the law to spread a rumor in Georgia, but only if it isn't true.

- In Corpus Christi, Texas, it's illegal to raise alligators in your home.

- It's against the law in Arkansas to blindfold cows on public highways.

Strange But True
The fear of long words is called hippopotomonstrosesquippedaliophobia.

Real Note Left on a Car Windshield
"The next time you park here & block me in I will monster truck your car into a pile of scrap."

@RodLacroix

I like to play 20 Questions with my kids but it's always me asking the questions and every question is "CAN YOU PLEASE FLUSH THE TOILET WHEN YOU'RE DONE?"

Bumper sticker:
TV Is Gooder Than Books

More English Subtitles from Hong Kong Action Movies

- "If you nag on, I'll strangle you with chewing gum."

- "A red moon? Why don't you say 'blue buttocks?'"

- "A poor band player I was, but now I am crocodile king."

- "Watch out! The road is very sweaty."

- "The wet nurse wants rock candy to decoct papayas."

From a real court transcript:
Q: Were you freebasing the cocaine?
A: No. I bought it.

Real Note Left on a Car Windshield
"You Park Like an A**hole.
Please Don't Reproduce."
(A condom was attached.)

Run for the Border

In 2003 *Men's Fitness* magazine named Houston "America's Fattest City." In response, a local group tried to change the city's image by holding a 40-mile bike rally through downtown Houston. But…to get people to sign up, they offered free beer and tacos at the finish line.

Great Moments in Dad History

September 8, 1995. Fred Small becomes the first known dad to clip his cell phone to his belt, kicking off a fashion trend that makes dads everywhere easily identifiable.

Bumper sticker:
Man cannot live on bread alone…unless he's in a cage and that's all you feed him.

MORE REAL COURT CASE NAMES

Muncher v. Muncher

People v. Booger

Short v. Long

State of Indiana v. Virtue

United States ex rel. Gerald Mayo v. Satan and His Staff

 @JaycubsWurld

Dad: Tall latte

Barista: Sure thing. Can I get a name?

Dad: What, your parents didn't give you one?

all the other dads give him high fives

Bumper sticker:
My wild oats have turned to shredded wheat

More Dumb Jock Quotes

"What defines me? Ryan Lochte."

—Ryan Lochte, Olympic swimmer

"I want to rush for 1,000 or 1,500 yards, whichever comes first."

—George Rogers, football player

"My career was sputtering until I did a 360 and got headed in the right direction."

—Tracy McGrady, basketball player

On a McDonald's sign:
Over 10 Billion Severed

More Ice Cream Flavors in Japan

Corn	Horseflesh
Wasabi	Goat
Eel	Shark fin and
Tulip	noodle
Mushroom	Seawater

Bumper sticker:
I used to have an open mind
but my brains kept falling out

Real note from a kid:
Sorry because of nothing

MORE LOONEY LAWS

• In Louisiana, a barber may not charge a bald man more than 25 cents for a haircut.

• It's against the law in Virginia to call someone on the telephone and not say anything.

• In Alaska, it's illegal to push a live moose out of a moving airplane.

• In French Lick Springs, Indiana, all black cats must wear bells on Friday the 13th.

• Women in Carrizozo, New Mexico, can't legally go out in public with hairy legs.

On a sign at a cake shop:
Cake Writting $2.00

66*Life would be tragic if it weren't funny.*99
—Stephen Hawking

FLUBBED HEADLINES

WOMAN IMPROVING AFTER
FATAL CRASH

Police to probe Barton's backside

**TV ads boost eating of
obese children by 130%**

*MEN THREATENED WITH GUNS WHILE
WORKING ON ONE OF THEM'S CAR*

**Legislator Wants Tougher
Death Penalty**

More English Subtitles from Hong Kong Action Movies

- "Cool! You really can't see the edges of the tea-bag underwear."

- "Beauty and charm is yours, to you I run. I'd never leave, even forced by gun. I'd always want you, even if you were a nun."

- "I scare nothing! Even you become napkins!"

- "Your dad is an iron worker, your mom sells beans!"

- "Same old rules: no eyes, no groin."

- "I'm Urine Pot the Hero!"

More Extremely Specific Online Dating Sites

CyclingSingles.com
Date-a-doc.com, for doctors
LawyersInLove.com
DatingForSmokers.com
MulletPassions.com
TrekPassions.com, for *Star Trek* fans
ShyPassions.com, for introverts

More Actual Job Titles According to the US Department of Labor

Frickerton Checker
Pickle Pumper
Retort Forker
Mutton Puncher
Human Projectile
Animal Impersonator

More Unfortunate Tattoo Fails

PROME QUEEN

NEVER LOOSE HOPE

It's get better

Regret Nohing

FAMILY IS EVERITHING

Your story i'snt lover yet

Towns With Odd Animal Names
(and we're pretty sure they don't have
anacondas or elephants)

Musk Ox, Alaska
Anaconda, Montana
Dinosaur, Colorado
Goat Town, Georgia
Toad Suck, Arkansas
Mastodon, Michigan
Wildcat, Wyoming
Elephant, Pennsylvania
Man, West Virginia

From a real court transcript:
Q: Meaning no disrespect, sir, but you're 80 years old, wear glasses, and don't see as well as you used to. So, tell me, just how far can you see?
A: I can see the Moon. How far is that?

Strange But True
Official state exercise of Maryland: walking

Game Show Goof
Bob Eubanks: What is your husband's favorite cuisine?
Contestant: *All in the Family.*

—*The Newlywed Game*

More Beer Names

Moose Drool
Men's Room Red
Yellow Snow
Mash of the Titans
Sweaty Betty
For Those About to Bock
Vampire Blood
Hoppy Ending

IF THEY MERGED

- If FedEx and UPS merged, the new company would be...*Fed-UP.*

- If Knott's Berry Farm and the National Organization for Women merged, they would become... *Knott-NOW.*

- If Grey Poupon and Dockers pants merged, they would be called...*Poupon Pants.*

- If Luvs diapers and Hertz car rental merged, the new company would be...*Luv Hertz.*

MORE REAL COURT CASE NAMES

• *United States v. $11,557.22 in U.S. Currency*

• *Advance Whip & Novelty Co. v. Benevolent Protective Order of Elks*

• *Fried v. Rice*

• *United States v. 1,100 Machine Gun Receivers*

• *Plough v. Fields*

Even More Ice Cream Flavors In Japan

Oyster	Curdled bean
Garlic mint	Silk
Sesame, soybean, and kelp	Collagen and lemon
	Pepto-Bismol

From a real court transcript:

Q: Ma'am, were you cited in the accident?
A: Yes, sir! I was so 'cited I peed all over myself!

When you oversleep and have to sneak into work late

What American TV Shows Were Called in Other Countries

U.S.: *Knight Rider*
Latin America: *The Fantastic Car*

U.S.: *Murder, She Wrote*
Germany: *Murder Is Her Hobby*

U.S. *SpongeBob SquarePants*
France: *Bob the Sponge*

More Euphemisms for Farting

Cheek squeak
Fanny beep
One-gun salute
Bottom blast
Barn burner
Beeping your horn
Fluffy
Message from the interior

 @HenpeckedHal

Crossing your fingers can symbolize telling a lie or praying for divine intervention. Either way, it perfectly sums up my parenting style.

Sign at a church:
The fact that there's a highway to Hell and only a stairway to Heaven says a lot about anticipated traffic numbers.

The 1984 movie *Dune* was adapted from a sci-fi novel that would not be considered kid-friendly. Its setting: a barren world is overrun with huge killer sandworms, a drug called spice is the currency of the universe, a global jihad is starting, and people are being assassinated. Naturally, the moviemakers thought it was prime subject matter for activity and coloring books for young kids. The connect-the-dots and coloring scenes depict "murder, intrigue, suppurating boils, phallic symbolism and knifeplay." Kids sure do grow up quick!

Cookie Monster's "real" name is Sid.

Even More Actual Job Titles According to the US Department of Labor

Lap Checker
Dobbyloom Chainpegger
Automatic Lump-Making Machine Tender
Soiled Linen Distributor
Muck Boss
Slubber Doffer
Gas Dispatcher

Nicknames of Medieval Kings

King Harald the Lousy
King Eric the Priest-Hater
King Henry the Impotent
King Baldwin the Leper
King Bermudo the Gouty
King Lulach the Foolish
King Vseslav the Werewolf
King Ethelred the Unready

Russian Slang Terms

Ne goní purgú!
Literally: "Don't chase away the snowstorm!"
Meaning: "Be honest!"

Ni khrená!
Literally: "Not a horseradish!"
Meaning: "Nothing of the kind!"

Gemorróy
Literally: "hemorrhoids"
Meaning: "a huge problem"

Blin!
Literally: "Pancake!"
Meaning: "Ah, shoot!"

"My mustache gets so many questions he has his own agent now."

—Tom Selleck

TABLOID HEADLINES

SEVERED LEG HOPS TO HOSPITAL

News reporter eaten alive by 80-ft. dinosaur

Aliens Passing Gas Caused Hole in Ozone Layer!

HOTCAKES NO LONGER SELLING WELL

Fountain of Youth Found in NYC Subway Toilet

Oatmeal Plant Blows Up; Omaha Buried in Icky Goo

L.A. QUAKE OPENS GATES OF HELL

Docs removed my BRAIN for NOTHING!

Q: What's the surest way to make any child extremely hungry and dehydrated?
A: Say, "It's bedtime."

 @HappyGrumpyDad

I love my kids despite everything. Who needs sleep, showers, privacy, clean clothes, time to yourself, hobbies, health or money anyway?

Wife: I've had it with your dumb dad jokes!
Husband: How can I quit?
Wife: Whatever means necessary.
Husband: No it doesn't!

Image Credits

5, 18, 40, 45, 202, 207 andrewgenn/iStock/Getty Images Plus • 7, 23, 111, 148, 261 leremy/iStock/Getty Images Plus • 8 and throughout boot Rizik_pic/iStock/ Thinkstock; beer, 13 drink, 140 sunnysideeggs/iStock/Thinkstock; football, 105, 177 dutchicon/iStock/Thinkstock; award, 13 award, 102 bubaone/DigitalVision Vectors/Getty Images • 9 Paul Bradbury/OJO Images/Getty Images • 10, 75 appleuzr/DigitalVision Vectors/Getty Images • 12 and throughout INchendio/ iStock/Getty Images • 13 and throughout shoe, lipstick Charlene Hea/iStock/ Getty Images Plus; watch nuranvectorgirl/iStock/Thinkstock • 14 AnnaNizami/ iStock/Getty Images • 21 Sophie Hogarth/Readerlink Distribution Services • 24, 227, 262 LueratSatichob/DigitalVision Vectors/Getty Images • 26, 53 Bakai/ iStock/Getty Images Plus • 28 JumlongCh/iStock/Getty Images Plus • 30, 62 bubble, 141, 253 bubble Bitter/iStock/Getty Images Plus • 36 ronstik/iStock/ Getty Images Plus • 41, 86, 159, 235 Nikiteev_Konstantin/iStock/Thinkstock • 49 AlonzoDesign/DigitalVision Vectors/Getty Images • 50 Valentin Amosenkov/ iStock/Getty Images Plus • 56 mushroomstore/iStock/Thinkstock • 62, 260 Bullet_Chained/iStock/Getty Images Plus • 68 traffic_analyzer/DigitalVision Vectors/Getty Images • 78, 97 leremy/iStock/Thinkstock • 80 cidepix/iStock/ Getty Images Plus • 83 Digital Vision./DigitalVision/Getty Images • 85 para827/ iStock/Getty Images Plus • 88 elmvilla/E+/Getty Images • 98, 122 VectOrOvich/ iStock/Getty Images Plus • 103 mecaleha/DigitalVision Vectors/Getty Images • 106, 163 Lina Topilina/iStock/Getty Images Plus • 127 ONYXprj/iStock/Getty Images Plus • 131 LokFung/DigitalVision Vectors/Getty Images • 132 Ulrik Tofte/ DigitalVision/Getty Images • 135 style-photography/iStock/Getty Images Plus • 138, 150, 165 kowalska-art/iStock/Thinkstock • 143, 285 youngID/DigitalVision Vectors/Getty Images • 145 briang77/iStock/Thinkstock • 146, 162 jameslee1/ DigitalVision Vectors/Getty Images • 147, 183 macrovector/iStock/Thinkstock • 152 browndogstudios/iStock/Thinkstock • 155 Kreatiw/iStock/Thinkstock • 156 GoodLifeStudio/E+/Getty Images • 166, 171, 189, 314 AnnIris/iStock/ Getty Images Plus • 176 man, 253 CSA-Archive/DigitalVision Vectors/Getty Images; bubble Alhontess/ iStock/Getty Images Plus • 179 lestyan4/iStock/Getty Images Plus • 186 Epine_art/iStock/Thinkstock • 187, 205 RyanJLane/E+/Getty Images • 196 Sudowoodo/iStock/Getty Images Plus • 201, 208, 218, 222, 230, 256, 258, 265 -VICTOR-/DigitalVision Vectors/Getty Images • 211, 248 appleuzr/ DigitalVision Vectors/Getty Images • 212 A-Digit/DigitalVision Vectors/Getty Images • 213 Thodoris_Tibilis/iStock/Getty Images Plus • 221 PeopleImages/ E+/Getty Images • 252 maglyvi/iStock/Getty Images Plus • 267 Image Source/ Photodisc/Getty Images • 270, 307, 318 oleksii arseniuk/iStock/Getty Images Plus • 275, 297 JakeOlimb/DigitalVision Vectors/Getty Images • 276 house shaunl/E+/Getty Images; gavel, 304 NatBasil/iStock/Thinkstock • 279 Jenyk/ iStock/Thinkstock • 282 miketarks/iStock/Getty Images Plus • 290 bulentgultek/ DigitalVision Vectors/Getty Images • 292 heart, 308 punsayaporn/iStock/ Getty Images Plus; ice cream Marina Parfenova/iStock/Getty Images Plus • 305 kaisorn/iStock/Thinkstock • 312 LKeskinen/iStock/Thinkstock • 317 milkal/iStock/Getty Images Plus